DECIDE & CONQUER

DECIDE&

CONQUER

44 Decisions That Will Make or Break All Leaders

DAVID SIEGEL

HARPERCOLLINS
LEADERSHIP

AN IMPRINT OF HARPERCOLLINS

Published by HarperCollins Leadership, an imprint of HarperCollins Focus LLC.

Any internet addresses, phone numbers, or company or product information printed in this book are offered as a resource and are not intended in any way to be or to imply an endorsement by HarperCollins Leadership, nor does HarperCollins Leadership vouch for the existence, content, or services of these sites, phone numbers, companies, or products beyond the life of this book.

ISBN 978-1-4002-3088-4 (eBook)

ISBN 978-1-4002-3087-7 (HC)

Library of Congress Control Number: 2021952499

Printed in the United States of America

22 23 24 25 26 LSC 10 9 8 7 6 5 4 3 2 1

To Lara, my life's best decision

CONTENTS

INTRODUCTION

Working with Adam Neumann provided all WeWork executives with an abundance of outlandish stories. A traditional pastime during offsites, in fact, was to swap Adam tales. My favorite of many encapsulates not just the man but the challenges I would have under him as chief executive officer of Meetup.

In January 2019, I was summoned from New York to San Francisco to have a one-on-one with Adam at WeWork's West Coast headquarters in Salesforce Tower. He began the meeting by telling me about what Meetup should evolve into. There was then a short break where Adam decided to shut the lights off and play *The Greatest Showman* in surround sound while he, myself, and the general manager from Latin America (I had no idea why he was there) sang along. The meeting was then interrupted by a critical call that Adam needed to make to confirm that the Samurai swords sent by Masayoshi Son (the largest investor in WeWork) had been delivered to Adam's home.

Then his wife, Rebekah, entered the room, promptly took off her shoes, and asked me who I was. Rebekah recently had been promoted to WeWork's chief brand officer. From my notes, our conversation went something like this:

Rebekah: Who are you?
David: The new CEO of Meetup.
Rebekah: What's Meetup?
Adam: We acquired Meetup a year ago.
Rebekah: We own Meetup? What do they do?

David (thinking): *The chief brand officer of WeWork doesn't even know they own us. Boy, I feel pretty damn unimportant.*

Rebekah: You should change the name of the company. It is terrible.

Adam: Well, they have built a brand for the last eighteen years, but we should definitely talk about changing the name.

David (thinking because he's speechless): *What the hell did I get myself into?!*

For those of you who are not one of the thirty million people who have attended a Meetup event since our founding in 2002, Meetup is the world's largest platform for finding and organizing community groups. The company's 300,000 groups in 193 countries create and host about 15,000 events every single day. Groups are organized geographically and meet online or in person around a shared interest, such as hiking, video games, or learning Java, or around a shared identity. Meetup groups are run by an organizer, who is charged a fee, and uses Meetup's online tools to set a time and place for the group's events, find new members, charge fees, screen potential members, upload photos, chat online, and more. Some groups are as small as three to five members and some have tens of thousands of members, but every group is its own unique community, with the potential to change the lives of its members. Meetup strives to drive both in-person connections and to use technology to connect people of shared interests and identities from around the world.

Meetup is a true public good and has bettered the lives of millions of its global members, as its founder, Scott Heiferman, intended when he founded the company following 9/11. He said:

I lived on Houston Street, and everything was shut down south of us for a few weeks. People in our apartment building started to make eye contact in a way that they never had before and they would ask you how you're doing. When people said hello to each other, you got this very palpable sense of community. . . . I had been the last person in the world to think that local community gatherings, or people turning to each other, are important. But this really hit me. . . . So then I started to read up on the topic. I came across Frances Cairncross's *The Death of Distance*, who says that in the cyber-future, distance won't matter anymore; you can be best friends with people in a sort of virtual world. But I was realizing just how important face-to-face was. Then I read Robert Putnam's "Bowling Alone: America's Declining Social Capital," where Putnam throws up this challenge of "How do you bring the parts of civil society that are really valuable into this twenty-first-century future?" And then I realized that what I should do is help people self-organize to form local communities.

In 2002, Scott raised $100,000 in angel funding and, later, $1.25 million in venture capital. The company launched its website in June 2002 and used these funds to organize events in thousands of cities across thousands of potential topics. Scott created millions of potential Meetup events by listing topics as far-ranging as Chihuahua lovers to ADHD support groups. No event would happen until at least four individuals responded that they would attend, and that would trigger an email to them that the event was a go. He then selected three locations as potential venues and had attendees select their preferred location. He made it as easy as possible to organize and attend events and seeded millions of potential opportunities. (See Mikolaj Jan Piskorski and David Chen, "Meetup," Harvard Business School Case 710-408, January 2010, revised February 2012.) Some 99 percent of those opportunities didn't trigger an event, but due to sheer volume, he needed a tiny fraction to succeed. And they did. Amazingly, Meetup attracted more than fourteen thousand users in its first month. Nine months later, the company had two hundred thousand users. By August 2003, the company grew to five hundred thousand users and fifteen hundred types of Meetup groups.

The tipping point for Meetup's growth was its political mobilization around the 2004 presidential election. Howard Dean became enamored with Meetup, and by September 2003 more than forty thousand Meetup members had attended a Howard Dean event. Dean's success resulted in both John Kerry and little-known Barack Obama using Meetup for their senatorial bids. Obama even promised that he would personally appear at any Meetup event in Illinois with more than one thousand RSVPs. In April 2005, the company made a major pivot and decided to start charging $9 per month to its organizers. Scott put a large notice on the website telling organizers, "We have some news to share that we don't think you're going to like." He was right. Meetup declined from fifty thousand groups to four thousand groups overnight and the company lost 90 percent of its activity. But the quality of Meetup groups went up substantially, and the percentage of successful Meetup events increased from 4 percent to 45 percent. That bold decision to drive quality over quantity saved Meetup from becoming a platform that no one trusted. It wasn't until 2009 that Meetup returned to more than fifty thousand groups, but at that point all its groups were led by paying organizers and hosting meaningful events around the world.

Meetup continued to grow revenue but was unable, or uninterested, in driving any meaningful profit. It was run more similarly to a nonprofit for years and reinvested any revenue growth that it realized. And then revenue started to flatten. Meetup needed to raise money again and, in the process of fundraising, found its suitor. Enter Adam

Neumann and WeWork. In November 2017, it was announced that Meetup would be acquired by WeWork for $156 million. Less than six months later, WeWork decided to find a new Meetup CEO.

That's where I came in.

A year after my meeting with Adam, WeWork was in free fall without a parachute, thanks to its disastrous IPO attempt, which exposed years of financial rot born of Adam's leadership. The company would slam into the ground a few months later due to COVID-19, which exposed its business model's obvious fatal flaw: What if people stopped needing offices?

The IPO nearly took down Meetup, and COVID could have also, seeing as we were a company dedicated entirely to facilitating in-person events at a time when you couldn't responsibly meet in person. But instead of failing, Meetup is now more profitable today than at any time in its eighteen-year history. And we are reinvesting that profit by meaningfully improving our organizer and member experiences. Meanwhile, Adam Neumann was replaced as CEO and WeWork left its space in Salesforce Tower.

Why did Meetup succeed while WeWork stumbled? It was in part because of our management team and some critical and company-defining decisions we made along the way.

That's a leader's primary job: making smart decisions. Even deciding what decisions to delegate and to whom are critical decisions. Leaders should make very few decisions, and for that reason, those decisions have an outsized impact. While every leader will base their decisions on their unique situation, history, and inclinations, the critical challenges all leaders face are invariably similar, starting with the first: Should you take the job as leader?

Other decisions include the following: What do you tell employees on day one? How can you build trust quickly with them? And whom should you trust yourself? Should you make changes quickly, say, to your executive team and the company strategy, or should you slow-play change to maintain stability? And how should you deal with your own boss, even if he's not erratic like Adam Neumann?

In all, I faced forty-four critical challenges at Meetup. These challenges are universal. As a new leader, you will face them too. It sounds like a lot, but they will come in manageable bursts: your first thirty days, the rest of your first quarter, your second quarter and the rest of your first year, then when your own major crisis inevitably strikes.

In this book I will walk you through how I navigated these challenges myself and came to the decisions I made—both right and wrong—in order to help you understand your options, manage your own hopes and fears, and thus make your own decisions easier and better.

And less fraught. Decision-making is hard enough. I think you'll find it comforting to know you're not alone as a leader in sometimes having doubts and feeling inadequate.

I hope you won't have to make your decisions amid the chaos of someplace like WeWork, which repeatedly blasted holes in our plans for future success, finally by deciding to sell us—and wanting to do so within a month—such that I had to go from saving Meetup for WeWork to saving Meetup from WeWork.

I have to say, though, that does make the story more interesting. So if you've come for the drama, great. But stay for the decisions. They'll make you a better leader.

1

GROUND RULES: BUILDING YOUR PERSONAL DECISION FRAMEWORK

Leaders bring to every decision a decision framework built from their earliest experiences and life lessons. So it's important for you to know my history and, thus, the framework I brought to the forty-four key challenges I faced at Meetup so you can see how you might have done things differently.

For instance, I used to be incredibly shy. Even afraid. In high school I was scared of roller coasters, terrified of swimming in a lake, and completely unable to speak in public. Speaking to a girl left me sweaty-palmed and incapable of putting two sentences together. My anxiety wasn't clinical; I just always felt nervous about exploring a new activity or meeting new people.

This changed the summer after I graduated. I was a counselor in a sleepaway camp, and for some inexplicable reason, a popular girl who was one of my fellow counselors gave all indications that she was interested in me. We spent countless evenings chatting and stayed in close touch during my upcoming precollege gap year. This relationship gave me confidence in myself, which let me reflect on who I was and how I'd been living. I didn't like it. I resolved not to be scared anymore. I would stand out and take risks, which is easy. Far harder to do, though, was facing why I had initially been shy and scared.

In elementary school, kids bullied me and called me names. One summer at camp I was given a wedgie. It was both physically and emotionally painful. Many of the kids whom I grew up with were assholes—and many later became adults who were assholes.

So the first leadership lesson I learned was to **be kind**.

I wouldn't be the same as those people. I wouldn't hurt others the way they did. However confident I got, I would remain empathetic, and this would eventually form the basis of my approach to leadership: Understanding employee needs. Sympathizing with their challenges. Motivating others to accomplish more than they thought they could. Treating people humanely and minimizing their pain, especially when they were vulnerable, such as during layoffs. That would be my life's calling.

My new capacity for risk turned into a desire for adventure, which led me to do the opposite of all of my Ivy League counterparts in college. While they took the most challenging classes, I took the easiest classes and put all my time and energy into learning outside of the classroom. I believed that my most transformative experiences became my greatest teachers. Humanity and life experiences taught me more than my classes.

Prior to 9/11 there were courier organizations where you gave up your luggage space in return for taking last-minute trips around the world on $99 flights. I did these often. During spring break of my freshman year in college, I called my mom from the airport, as I had found an immediate flight to Belgium that week. She was wondering why I was sleeping so late (I had come home for spring break) and she hadn't heard from me that morning. I slept on rooftops in Jordan, sold CD players on the streets of Israel, taught English to Russian immigrants in Brighton Beach and Hebrew to Ukrainians in Ukraine. I would open a falafel stand in NYC, attend the religious ceremonies of Moonies, Hare Krishnas, and Shakers, and generally find any opportunity to experience something completely different than others. And this while I was still a teenager. I learned the importance of **being confident**, but never cocky, in making smart decisions.

Toward the end of my sophomore year at the University of Pennsylvania, I went to a student conference at Princeton and ended up sleeping on a random student's floor. I asked him what he was doing after he graduated and he told me he was going to become a consultant. He told me it was the perfect job for someone who didn't know anything but had the confidence to pretend like he knew everything. Sign me up.

This was prior to the internet, too, so I asked him to fax me the "golden list" he'd cobbled together of the one hundred largest consulting firms in the United States. I sent each firm my resume, which might as well have been a blank piece of paper, and eagerly awaited the rush of job offers. Instead, I received one hundred rejections, but at least they responded!

Then I received a phone call from Mercer Management Consulting. While their New York office had rejected me, they'd sent my letter to their Philadelphia office. Turns out I was the perfect candidate for them—because no one else had applied to be their intern. I got the job without an interview and spent the summer soliciting pharmaceutical companies to participate in their annual human resources survey. I enjoyed making a salary and decided to work there again during the school year. Failure and rejection from nearly every consulting firm taught me the importance of taking initiative and not following the standard path. I also learned the "law of large numbers," which boils down to the larger the volume of opportunities you pursue, the greater the number of opportunities you will have. People look for perfection and thereby create fewer potential opportunities for themselves. Instead, embrace imperfection and you'll have more and better future options. I also saw the rewards if I resolved to **be confident**.

The confidence I developed rippled forward from there and enabled me in all things to **be bold**.

I have never gotten a job that I was an ideal candidate for. At all times there were many individuals who knew more and would likely do a better job than I. I never cared. I genuinely believed that the company was lucky to have me leading the team, and I would find a way to succeed.

It would ultimately allow me to believe that I could engineer the acquisition of Meetup out of WeWork no matter the odds. I never wavered in my confidence, not only that we would succeed but that there was no better leader for the company. Perhaps it's because as a white man, I have a great deal of privilege that empowers me to challenge rules, expectations, and norms. I recognize that this makes it much easier for me to ignore "do not enter" signs and flout convention in a way that isn't available to others. (I am heartened by the conversations happening within our society to recognize the impact of privilege in corporate structures. I orient my own actions to influence others and ensure all people have these opportunities, as I deeply wish.) When friends tell me they don't think they are ready for a certain position and that a role is bigger than they deserve, I tell them the bigger the role, the better. If you succeed, great. If you fail, and over time you likely will, even better. If you fail, you'll learn more. Get the gig, then figure out how to do it.

The same could be said of maximizing opportunities.

Students are often taught the importance of building a specialty and taking a focused approach in their career choices. But this focus results in fewer and sometimes no choices, which then limits the likelihood a student will find a role that is the best fit for their specific needs. Besides, how many students even know what they want and what they'll need when they get to college?

I had taken classes in twenty different fields by the time I was a junior, and I still had no idea what I wanted to do. I couldn't even imagine specifically focusing on any one topic and not trying to maximize my interest in building broad experiences. The University of Pennsylvania then decided to offer a new interdisciplinary major called PPE (philosophy, political science, and economics). I wouldn't need to limit myself, as I didn't believe in self-imposed limits. I could have a non-major major—and I ended up becoming the first PPE graduate from the University of Pennsylvania. The lessons were an inch deep and a mile wide; that is, I had a cocktail party level of knowledge about everything. I would become the specialist in nothing but have basic skills across broad disciplines, and most important, I'd be able to understand the relationship between disciplines, which is often the best approach to tackling problems.

Turns out, this was the ideal preparation for being a CEO. I am an expert in very little. Each one of my direct reports knows more than I about their area of functional expertise. My priority is understanding the interdisciplinary reason for a challenge. If we have a sales challenge, it isn't solely a sales challenge. It is also likely a product, marketing, or incentive challenge. If our product isn't meeting the needs of our users, it isn't just a product issue but likely related to our approach to editorial, research, design, or engineering. Nothing is one-dimensional. As I learned from my earlier years, understanding others' perspectives allows a leader to understand the myriad bases for company challenges and to make decisions across an organization rather than focusing on one function.

Instead of trying one thing at a time, try a lot of things at the same time. Keep what works and ditch the rest. **Expand your options.** You'll see yourself finding more success. Convention has always dictated the importance of specialization. David Epstein's 2019 book *Range: Why Generalists Triumph in a Specialized World* has dispelled the convention of specialization. Seriously playing a diversity of sports at a young age has been demonstrated to accelerate an athlete's elite performance, and the same holds true for the value of diverse experiences for business leaders.

The serendipity that comes from the optionality of diverse work experiences will drive more success than a persistent and potentially myopic focus of specialization. The risk of having many opportunities

is, of course, being unable to choose among them and thereby losing all of them. Decision paralysis can impact every aspect of your
personal and professional life. What worked for me was reminding
myself to **focus on the long-term picture**. A decision isn't just about
the challenge at hand. It should help you overcome (or at least better
set you up to overcome) challenges down the road on the way toward
your larger goals.

For instance, I wasn't sure whether I'd enjoy consulting after college, so I decided to get as many job offers as I could. And because
I'd worked for a human resources consulting firm, the best way to do
that would be to apply to other human resources consulting firms.

I ended up with four offers. Three were from large, prestigious
brand names with established career paths. The other was from
Brecker & Merryman, a forty-person firm that had never hired anyone straight out of college but told me I would get the same level of
experience as the three MBAs they hired. I accepted quickly because
my goal wasn't a job. It was experience so I could decide whether I
wanted that sort of job.

There my biggest client was DoubleClick, one of the first internet
companies in New York. DoubleClick's stock had increased more
than 500 percent over the prior year and the company was in the
throes of the "internet bubble." True to Brecker & Merryman's word,
and thanks to their lack of hierarchy, I was given significant exposure
to the company's management team instead of being a backroom
PowerPoint drone, like most twenty-three-year-old analysts. I quickly
built a relationship with DoubleClick CEO Kevin Ryan.

He was on a hiring frenzy and one day asked me what I was making. When he realized that he could pay me close to double my current
salary and that would be less than half of what my consulting firm
was billing for me, he offered me the newly created role of human
resources partner at DoubleClick. I was fortunate to have built a personal relationship with Kevin when consulting to DoubleClick and

that relationship led directly to this opportunity. And I had that exposure only because I had specifically chosen a consulting firm that would prioritize direct client exposure over a big-brand consultancy. I gladly accepted, although I had absolutely no idea what I was supposed to do in that role. But I would get experience.

DoubleClick was a dream. I couldn't believe that at twenty-four years old I was already managing someone and in one of the most impactful companies in the nascent internet economy. Then the bubble burst and my 401(k) was full of DoubleClick stock. I had a front-row seat to watching my retirement fund decrease by more than 80 percent.

That was only part of the nightmare. As an HR partner for our tech business, I was then asked to terminate thirty employees in one day, as part of a layoff of more than two hundred and fifty employees. And I had to handle the entire process for my division on my own.

But this is exactly what I'd signed up for. This experience. Fewer than 1 percent of CEOs ever worked in human resources departments, but more should. Anne Mulcahy, Xerox's former chairman and CEO, and Jeff Brodsky, Morgan Stanley's vice chairman, are in a very small class of individuals who rose through the human resources ranks to lead their organizations. Kevin Ryan once told me, "What you and I do is pretty similar. We need to focus on recruiting top talent, motivating employees, providing the right performance incentives, and building strong management teams."

I believe HR provided a framework for how I wanted to lead organizations and build a company culture—with a people-first approach, especially when, twenty years later, I would have to lay off people from Meetup. And from that experience I learned what I needed to. I didn't want to be a consultant. I needed to be more involved, roll up my sleeves, and not create binders or PowerPoint decks that never went anywhere. For similar reasons, I did not want to stay in HR. HR tends to be internally focused and lacks exposure to external customers, product, marketing, or sales. I had to move on to gain the skills needed to achieve my long-term goal, which, I decided, was being a CEO. At this point I had only two opportunities: a sales position at Double-Click or a slot at Wharton business school. It wasn't an easy decision. The sales position would offer me a total compensation package that was greater than the average Wharton MBA salary. I had just had my first child and my wife wanted to leave her job and focus on taking care of our son.

I sought advice from David Rosenblatt. David was the general manager of a business unit at DoubleClick, and I was a human resources partner at that time. We had worked together on figuring out different people-related strategies for the business. David had gone to business school and advised me that the education I would get from Wharton would be more valuable long term than the increased short-term compensation.

Following David's advice, I decided to focus on the long-term gain, not the short-term pain, and returned to Penn. We went from two salaries for two people to zero salary for three people, for two years. I had to take more than $100,000 in loans, but I always had the confidence that, by being bold, things would work out in the end.

Ultimately, David was absolutely right. I look back very fondly on that decision. There have been at least ten decisions throughout my career where he was the first person I called for advice. He's on the board of Twitter and IAC and is the CEO of 1stDibs. More important, he remains an exceptional mentor, person, and friend. I hadn't realized it at the time, but I had started to assemble my personal board of advisors, which would prove to be instrumental to my career. Jim Collins, the author of *Good to Great*, has been one of the most vocal advocates of the impact of your personal board of advisors. He wrote that the "process of assembling and making good use of a personal board is a conscious, deliberate step toward answering the question:

what kind of person do you want to be and what vision do you aspire to?" Everyone should build a personal board.

I was ready to leave DoubleClick, but the company wasn't yet done with me. Before I left, CEO Kevin Ryan forced me into a decision that would teach me something as valuable as always being kind. During our goodbye meeting he said, "Hey, you've got nothing to lose at this point. You're leaving next week. Give me some honest advice on our executive team."

I knew exactly what I needed to say about two members of his team, but what would it say about me, burning them, however deservedly, while I headed for the door? It wouldn't be kind. So what would that then mean for my relationship with Kevin? Because I did have something to lose: my reputation. He did ask, though, and I trusted him, so I decided to **be honest**—brutally, when necessary. Try to live by the principle that Jack Stack established in *The Great Game of Business*: "A business should be run like an aquarium, where everybody can see what's going on."

I told him that there were several senior executives that had been speaking disparagingly about him to their teams. It was leading to a dysfunctional executive team, and I didn't care how strong they were as functional leaders, they had to go.

They were fired by the end of the week.

This taught me to cultivate honest assessments. While all leaders should get together with employees whom they trust prior to their leaving and get unfiltered advice, making that practice a regular occurrence might keep them from leaving. I also learned how influential one can be without any specific power or responsibility.

Wharton was an important experience for a different reason than why most people pursue business school. I literally knew nothing about business and wanted to learn the trade. I focused solely on building hard skills in marketing, finance, and quantitative analysis, having a lot of soft management skills already. In 2003, I was graduating from Wharton and had no interest in following the path of the vast majority of my classmates and going into finance or consulting. Having thought about the most meaningful learning opportunities of my career, all came from mentors. I decided that because I wanted to eventually become a CEO myself, my ideal post–business school job was to be mentored directly by a CEO and to become an assistant to the CEO. You may not be familiar with this role. Many CEOs aren't. I wasn't looking to be an executive assistant, managing the CEO's schedule and booking travel. I wanted to work on strategic projects directly for the CEO, build a deep relationship with a CEO, and learn as much as I could from our daily interactions.

The challenge, of course, was that no such role existed in 99 percent of companies. I needed to create and sell a new role and thereby sell myself. So I proceeded on an unlikely path with an unlikely strategy. I identified about fifty companies of interest. I found a database that listed the top thirty executives at each company. I was able to figure out what each company's email was (dsiegel@ . . . , david.siegel@ . . . , etc.) and then use an Excel merge function to create the two thousand email addresses for the top executives at each of the fifty companies. My goal was massive volume to get introductions directly to the company's CEO.

I would take a high-volume, low-quality approach once again. Over one evening in March, I sent out all two thousand emails—better to **be speedy** to see what works and doesn't so I could get to the next steps. I ended up connecting one-on-one with at least ten of those CEOs: Ken Chenault, the CEO of American Express; David Stern, the commissioner of the NBA; David Neeleman, the CEO of JetBlue; and Jim McCann, the CEO of 1-800-Flowers.com, among others. It was this massive blitz that not only led to my first job out of business school— working for the CEO and running business development for Duane Reade, but also my following job as an executive at 1-800-Flowers.com.

But at first, my strategy was a total failure.

I couldn't get a single company to hire me as an assistant to the CEO. The Boston Consulting Group (BCG) offered me a job as a "senior consultant," a standard post–business school title—and I was informed that my start date had been pushed to January 2004. It was May 2003. I was graduating. I was $100,000 in debt, was given a start date in eight months, and told I could travel the world until my start date. Sounds great, except my kid needed to eat.

So I had to do something I'd decided against: I accepted the job offer from the Boston Consulting Group. I should have been less reluctant and more grateful. BCG was one of the "big three" elite consulting firms and most every MBA student would kill to work there. But to make sure I could take care of my family, I decided I had to **be pragmatic**.

While this was a step off the road I planned to take, I kept looking down it. I was able to persuade the CEO of Duane Reade to let me do a six-month paid internship. After six months, the company asked me to stay and not leave for BCG. I accepted quickly and then called the BCG partner and told him that I would be rescinding my acceptance.

He began to fume on the phone and screamed, "You're making a huge mistake. No one turns down BCG! You're never going to work in consulting again!" OK, I wanted to say.

Then he asked me what I was going to be doing and I said, "I'll be running business development for Duane Reade." There was a long pause before he asked, "Well, do you feel guilty enough that maybe you can recommend us for a consulting opportunity there?" Had he been kinder, he could have gotten a new client.

Having prioritized myself over BCG in accepting, then refusing their offer, I found myself in the same position at Duane Reade, deciding whether I should do what was right for me over what was right for the company.

Duane Reade had a long-standing consumer problem: It was a pain in the ass for people to wait in line at a pharmacy, drop off a prescription, then either wait or return to pick up their medication. So the CEO and I developed a new technology called Duane Reade Express, similar to an airline kiosk. Through very early videoconferencing technology, individuals could speak to a pharmacist and scan their prescriptions and then have the prescription delivered to their home or have it ready for immediate pickup in any Duane Reade store. I hired sales, support, and tech teams to build these kiosks and place them in physician offices, senior living facilities, company headquarters, and hospitals. We then gave the machines away for free and saw increased prescriptions from each location.

While at its height the kiosks were processing thousands of prescriptions a week, the technology was too early to gain widespread consumer adoption and it frequently broke down. It was also too costly to produce and run a network of kiosks around New York City where the chain was founded and based.

If I couldn't make the system work, I'd likely be out of a job, which gave me every incentive to build a new business regardless of whether or not it was a good business.

Although there were serious business and technology issues, I pushed for continued rapid expansion of the program and convinced myself that greater volume would drive efficiency and eliminate our losses. (Note: This very rarely works, as every startup that tries to scale too early discovers very quickly.) Had we started slower, and continued to refine the technology instead of scaling it, we would have had greater success, but I did what was right for me when I should have been honest with myself, faced facts, and **done what was right for the business**. When a new CEO was brought in, he decided to cease all expansion, and I decided to quickly find another job. Thus, I made the wrong decision in prioritizing scaling over efficiency.

Fortunately, the job I'd always wanted was suddenly there for the taking.

A Wharton classmate told me that 1-800-Flowers.com had posted a new job on Wharton's alumni database. The name of the job: assistant to CEO—with the exact job description I had tried to sell the CEO on three years prior. I was shocked, so I emailed the CEO to say, "You may not remember me, but a few years ago I tried to convince you to hire me as your assistant. If for some reason that influenced your decision to look for an assistant, I would love to catch up." His response was five words long: "I was looking for you." He might as well have said: "You had me at hello." My one-night blitz of thousands of emails to executives back in 2003 had paid off.

I was twenty-nine and hired as a vice president at 1-800-Flowers .com. At thirty-two, I was promoted to be a senior vice president. By thirty-five, I was asked to lead a division of Everyday Health, and then at thirty-eight, I became president of Seeking Alpha. Upon turning forty, I went to Investopedia to finally fulfill my career aspiration and become a CEO.

So now what? For twenty years, my mission had been my career. Going forward, I decided it would be the careers of my employees. **Work for them, and they'll work for you.**

I had always wanted to be a CEO because I saw how deeply a CEO impacted an organization. The CEO built the culture, and a company's culture determined whether the company would succeed or fail. I swore that I would muster every learning experience from the early days of my career in human resources and build the most amazing company culture that any employee had ever been a part of. And we did.

We succeeded because we built a team galvanized by our mission to be the world's largest financial education website.

Employees loved working at Investopedia. For three years, we had an annual retention rate of over 90 percent and were named one of the

100 Best Places to Work in New York City by *Crain's*, a Top Company by *Fortune*, and for three straight years as the Top Publisher to Work For by Business Intelligence Group. This drove business success, which then drove employee motivation further as we saw the results of our hard efforts paying off. This motivation drove further business success. It was a positive feedback loop.

As a result, in three years the company went from 26 employees and zero revenue growth to 150 employees and more than triple the revenue. We felt invincible—which is the exact time that we should have felt most vulnerable.

And that's how I stopped being CEO.

Partially due to our success, coupled with our parent company's need to consolidate its businesses, I received a call one day to meet with the head of the publishing group and was promptly informed that the company had been sold to Dotdash, a sister company in IAC's portfolio. They paid a substantial amount above Investopedia's valuation when I started and a far higher multiple than what IAC (Investopedia's parent company) had initially paid to acquire it. Yay.

There was no due diligence. I had no warning. And I was told to inform our employees the very next day.

Neither the death of family members nor the shock of world events impacted me as much as this conversation. I was literally catatonic. I had poured my heart and soul into the company. We had succeeded in every conceivable way and I was out. I couldn't muster the energy to take on another role. I asked for and received a severance, but that couldn't make up for the loss I felt.

I learned a lot. I learned that all jobs are just jobs. We should put everything we can into succeeding, but enduring the ending is rarely a positive experience. I learned that doing a good job is a true reward in and of itself. It's not about the outcome but the careers of employees and impact on individuals one can have in a job. As Wayne Dyer, the self-help guru and author of over thirty books, said, "When you dance, your purpose is not to get to a certain place on the floor. It's to enjoy each step along the way." I also learned that anything can happen at any time and **the only thing to be surprised about is actually being surprised about anything**. This last learning experience served me better than any other lesson when it came to managing the tumultuous six months of Meetup's roller-coaster sale out of WeWork.

Not foreseeing the sale, having created the ideal conditions for one, was a big mistake, but it was hardly my only one.

I have made my share of mistakes, and they have resulted in millions if not tens of millions of dollars lost and hundreds of employees terminated. I'm neither proud of nor ashamed of these mistakes; they most often exist as inevitable consequences of either personal insecurities, inexperience, and for some, inappropriate motivations. They have been often compounded by larger industry dynamics, but the root cause of these failures was solely my actions. I'd like to share a few, since I have gained far more from these failures than from my successes, and I am hopeful the reader will as well.

One mistake I made was scaling a business for personal gain instead of there being a clear product-market fit. Often the incentives of a leader are divergent from the incentives of a company. It is critical for leaders to recognize this dynamic. A company may be focused on massive growth while the leader just wants to retain their job. This results in a far more risk-averse behavior that doesn't drive toward the company's priorities. Alternatively, as in the case earlier in my career at Duane Reade, I was focused on growing my career, building a big business, and gaining the experience of managing significant numbers of people. The company was looking to minimize risks. I was looking to maximize my experience. Oftentimes it is the leader, not the company, who ends up getting their way and the company "catches up" and takes action only years later.

I failed as a general manager at Everyday Health for nearly the exact same reason. What is even more inexcusable was my not learning from the mistakes I had made at Duane Reade. At Everyday Health I was hired to build a new business connecting local physicians to the company's network of thirty million health-focused users. Had I tried to start this business from scratch, it would have taken many years to build meaningful revenue. My only path to success—and staying employed—was to acquire a company. I pushed hard for a deal and we overpaid for it. My need to urgently prove myself resulted in an acquisition that cost Everyday Health more than $10 million more than they finally sold it for years later. It also resulted in hiring up to 150 employees only to be asked to reduce our staff to 50 as the company made the decision to go public. When I put my name on the list and got what I most deserved, it was the first time I was fired.

Another example of a serious failure was when I was CEO of Investopedia. I had regarded myself as invincible due to the company's growth and success. I focused on creating a company culture of fun, and every week for three years, I organized a crazy relay race between employees. Think of every silly summer camp game, corporate retreat outing, or YouTube video. Whether it was eating contests, scavenger hunts, plank contests, you name it. We had these zany activities once a week, for about fifteen minutes each week. It was fully optional for anyone to participate, and no one was ever forced to do so. However, a small group of employees didn't enjoy these games. Looking back, I believe it created a fraternity- or sorority-type environment and led to others' discomfort. No one should ever feel discomfort when they come to work. The work environment needs to be a safe and inclusive space for people to be their authentic selves. I pushed too hard on the "fun" and failed those employees who felt uncomfortable with the frivolity. Leaders need to find the right balance of creating environments for their employees to really enjoy coming to work while at the same time ensuring it is a safe and inclusive space for everyone.

Leaders lead by building tool kits that they have developed throughout their personal and professional lives.

As the CEO of Meetup, I implemented each of the lessons from my life and career prior to Meetup over and over again. I often didn't need to think about what decision to make when I joined the company and as we were getting sold; my decision was simply an automatic one and the result of forty-four years of how I had led my life to that point.

Here is a summary of my decision framework—a framework we will continue to go back to—as it relates to making optimal decisions:

- Be kind.

- Be confident.

- Be bold.

- Expand your options.

- Be long-term focused.

- Be honest.

- Be speedy.

- Be pragmatic.

- Do what's right for the business.

- Work for your employees.

- Be surprised only about being surprised.

2

YOUR WEEK 0 CHALLENGE

Being a good leader boils down to one thing: responding to challenges by making good decisions.

Your particular background will inform these decisions, which is why I wanted you to know mine so you could see what led to the decisions I have made during my time at Meetup. I expect you'll think I was wrong in some cases based on your own particular background, and in other cases your background may have led you to reach an even better decision. This is fine, and often you will be correct in that assessment. I only hope that my decisions—and the process by which I reached them—helps you address your own career and leadership challenges.

I have identified forty-four key challenges that I faced at Meetup. These challenges are universal. Anyone who takes on a leadership role will face them in some form. In fact, the first challenge you'll have to address comes before you're even hired. I call this Challenge 0 since it is technically a challenge before you even begin. So, think of this as a bonus to the forty-four key decisions!

Challenge 0: Should you take the job?

Decision 0: Put in the work to make the right choice

This is not as easy a decision as it sounds, and it's an even harder one if the job sounds great. Because then you have to decide: Is this a great job on paper, perhaps with a title I want to have, or is this the right job for me? So put in the work to reach the right decision. It may be your most important, especially if you're deciding whether to work for a unicorn like WeWork.

Every job in my career came as a direct or indirect result of a prior relationship I had built. I've never applied for a new role, I've only been introduced by someone to a new opportunity. I don't intentionally maintain relationships with people who can "help me in the future." Instead, I maintain relationships with people whom I genuinely like and respect and whose company I enjoy. It's easy to weed out those who clearly care about me only because of what I might someday be able to do for them. Don't maintain relationships for selfish reasons; maintain them because they help you be your authentic self. **Be confident.**

Personal relationships had a different meaning at WeWork. The founder and CEO of Meetup, Scott Heiferman, didn't know WeWork was looking for his replacement until a friend of his was contacted about the job—despite Adam Neumann having promised Scott that if he were to ever replace him, he would tell him directly. I later asked Adam about this, and Adam, the type of person who runs to confrontations the way dogs run to hydrants, said he'd made a terrible mistake by avoiding a confrontation with Scott. As a result, he felt it was critical to ensure that not only would Scott need to approve of the CEO hire, but that Scott needed to stay with the company, *reporting to the new CEO.*

I didn't know Scott, but that sounded insane. Scott was Meetup's only CEO in its sixteen-year history. He was the heart and soul of the company, and while he was both beloved by most and disliked by some, it would be impossible for a new CEO to operate with the flexibility needed to change a company's culture, strategy, and priorities with the founder a part of the management team.

I have been asked often what it's like to interview with a maverick like Adam Neumann. And my answer is always the same: "It's exactly as you would have thought. Insane." Adam didn't ask about my past work experiences. Most of my interview was about family and spirituality. I was given a tour of his private ice bath and sauna (which he apparently would use at 5 or 6 a.m.) and was offered a full-course Israeli vegan spread. While we had a meaningful conversation about life, Adam wasn't convinced that I was the right person to lead Meetup. So, I decided that if given the opportunity for a second interview, I would up my game and channel my inner Adam Neumann. Leaders like to hire leaders like themselves, and if I were to get the job, it would be because Adam would find me similar to himself. Having Adam as an employer, you had to be prepared for anything. **Be surprised only about being surprised.**

A few weeks later, as I walked into WeWork for my second interview with Adam, I spotted a young employee wearing a T-shirt that said "Meetup + WeWork." I was wearing a white dress shirt. Adam surely wouldn't be, so I decided I needed that shirt. I approached the employee and explained that I was interviewing for the Meetup CEO job and that I'd like his shirt. We went into a closet and I traded my Brooks Brothers button-down for a ragged tee. When Adam saw me, he said, "Man, if you can convince someone to give you the shirt off their back, then you can sell anything." As I had learned earlier: **Be bold.**

WeWork made the decision to hire me, but Adam communicated that he wanted Scott and Meetup's executive team to feel that I was their choice and not WeWork's choice. So, after fifteen interviews with WeWork leaders, I needed to start the process over and have another twelve conversations with Meetup executives.

Three of those would be with Scott. The first went OK. The second, better. Still unconvinced, he wanted to meet a third time, this time for half a day. I understood that the problem wasn't me personally. After sixteen years at the helm, it seemed like he wasn't about to turn it over to someone he barely knew. So he took me to Meetup events around New York City to show me the mission of Meetup in action.

We first visited an early-morning soccer game in Brooklyn, where I spoke with a new member of the group who had just moved from Germany. He missed the group of friends he'd played soccer with every week. Thanks to Meetup, he now had twenty new friends to play with and afterward join at the pub.

Our next stop was a daily event hosted in a WeWork conference room, a chance to see their synergies in action. I listened in as nearly a dozen women who were all working on their PhDs strengthened and supported each other during what is often an incredibly painful and lonely task.

We then headed to Central Park where I met the founder of City Dads, one of the most successful Meetup groups. Many stay-at-home dads had felt marginalized going to mommy-and-me classes and looked to meet other guys in a similar situation to their own. The bonding was awesome and inspirational. Even more amazing was that the group had expanded to more than thirty chapters across the United States and abroad, because when the dads moved they started City Dad Meetup groups in their new cities.

I saw firsthand the growth potential of this very special company. I also realized what a powerful force Scott could be going forward by taking new hires out on similar field trips. It was a wonderful experience.

Then reality struck. Scott, apparently still unconvinced I was the one, asked me to have dinner with the entire Meetup leadership team, each of which I'd already met with, and I had to decide whether it was time to put my foot down and say, *No. Put up or shut up.*

I had already spent more than three hundred hours preparing for, traveling to, participating in, and following up after each of my interviews. I felt I was being taken advantage of and at the whim of a founder who was unable (or unwilling) to step aside. On top of that, while they'd been struggling to decide whether I was a good fit for them, I'd been struggling to decide if they were a good fit for me.

As the process dragged on, I had to keep asking myself whether I wanted to accept because I had put such enormous time and energy into interviewing or because I truly wanted the job. Failing to appreciate the sunk cost fallacy had led me to make poor decisions previously because I view "wasted time" as such a vice. Plus, momentum favored me taking the job. It's tough to stop and reconsider your options when things are moving fast, especially if you also like to win. And if I took the job, I wouldn't just be CEO. I'd have beaten out dozens of other impressive candidates and emerged victorious. So I needed to appreciate the fact that whether or not I took the Meetup job, the hundreds of hours I'd spent were gone, and I should make the right decision for me.

I also worried whether rejecting the job would reflect negatively on Michael Eisenberg, the WeWork board advisor who recommended me for the role. And I worried how it would reflect negatively on me. Would the WeWork and Meetup executives I had met consider me duplicitous and untrustworthy and want nothing more to do with me? **Be honest.**

These reasons weren't reasons to take a job either. If your friend recommended you for a job, and you found out it would entail jumping off a bridge, should you do it? No. Again, you have to look past the various cognitive biases that come into play when trying to get a big job, such as the sunk cost fallacy and the winner's curse, and focus on the job itself. You're always better off rejecting a role than accepting it for the wrong reasons.

Fortunately, I had my own history to guide me. Three years earlier, Investopedia asked me to be their CEO, a job I'd been working toward for fifteen years, and I initially decided no.

I told Joey Levin, CEO of IAC (Investopedia's parent company), that I couldn't make an educated decision because I hadn't gone on any other interviews. I didn't know what else was out there for me, or what I was worth on the market. I said, "I feel like I would be marrying the first person I dated if I took this job."

To explore my options, I then left my job as president of Seeking Alpha, and made it my full-time job to "find the best job for me." The "for me" was critical because, as you might have guessed, the job at Seeking Alpha had looked great on paper but wasn't right for me. Before falling into the same trap, I would talk with leaders I trusted, taking stock of what I loved and hated in my career. I ended up meeting with hundreds of companies and receiving two other executive job offers before I went back to Joey Levin and said, "Hey, I know it's been three months, but I'm ready to make a decision." I'll admit that went well beyond being bold to being ballsy. For all I knew, the position was no longer available or, if it was, they were sufficiently pissed off at my having rejected the offer that they wouldn't even return my call. **Expand your options.**

Their response: "We're about to give the offer to someone else. But we still prefer you. If you want the role, it is yours, but you cannot reject it again." I asked my future boss to meet again so we could talk it out. Joey agreed.

The trick to interviews, I've found, isn't what you say. It's what you can get interviewers to say, because, in my experience, they can do only one of two things at a time. They can either evaluate you or sell you on their organization. You want them doing the latter. It has always astounded me how appealing I can suddenly seem to be as a candidate after I've flipped the switch by, for example, voicing concerns and asking to learn more about my future employer. In this case, I set the pros and cons of this role against those of the other two I'd been offered. At Investopedia I'd be the final decision-maker, I'd build the culture instead of just being part of it, and I knew the business cold thanks to my previous job at their competitor, Seeking Alpha. One of the competing offers would pay more, despite my only being a GM. Joey then spent more time selling me on the role, becoming more confident that I was the right leader. I took the job. I chose to give up short-term financial gain for the experience of being the final decision-maker and culture builder. **Be long-term focused.**

Drawing on this experience, I decided to trust my own judgment in accepting the job if Meetup offered it but conversely felt that I could reject the position without getting hurt. And, thanks to my tour of events with Scott, I decided I really did want the job since Meetup's mission had personally resonated with me. Like the German soccer player, I knew loneliness. I had also experienced the joys of being part of rich and vibrant communities: my synagogue, my kids' school, my neighborhood. It saddened me that these kinds of communities weren't accessible to everyone.

I also believe that work should be meaningful because life is too short. When I was twenty-four, my best friend, Alan Helmreich, passed away from a shocking brain aneurysm. Two months later, another friend died by suicide. Then my father died. You spend more of your waking hours working than any other activity. You spend more time on the job than with your spouse or kids. My grief showed me that, if possible, no one should waste this time on something that didn't make an impact.

And at Meetup I could have a global impact.

Nonetheless, at the risk of blowing everything up, I told WeWork that I wouldn't go on another meeting with anyone. I was done. If they wanted to hire me, they should make me an offer or let me know they were going in another direction.

And they offered me the job, which I would accept—with three conditions.

One of my core beliefs is that if there is an opportunity to negotiate, take it. Don't worry about looking too financially driven. It is that worry that has kept millions of leaders from negotiating aggressively.

I've always believed that not only is it not a negative reflection to negotiate compensation, it's actually a negative reflection to *not* ask for it. Never be shy about negotiating your compensation. **Be confident.**

When I accepted a general manager role at Everyday Health about ten years prior, I learned a great lesson from my boss and founder of the company, Ben Wolin. Ben would often do the direct salary negotiations with executives whom he hired. I was particularly aggressive in a number of my requests. After the contract negotiation, I asked Ben if he was put off by my aggressive negotiating. Ben responded, "When I hire executives, I like to see how strong they are in advocating for themselves, how willing they are to debate and compromise, and their confidence in themselves. If an executive isn't going to push for a higher salary and benefits for themselves"—or push to stop an endless interview process, I should add—"then they won't push for a key company priority, which likely has less of an impact on them."

My first ask of Artie Minson, WeWork's president and chief financial officer, was that I wanted to confirm that I wouldn't be reporting to Adam Neumann. Adam had told me during the interview process that he'd plan to spend one day a month with me at Meetup. That was too much. Even one visit seemed too much. I had nothing against Adam, I was truly awed by him in fact, but it became clear that he had very strong opinions about how Meetup should be run, and I needed a buffer between Adam and me to provide support toward where I wanted to take the company. Artie agreed. What actually happened: Adam never visited even once while I was CEO. I was beckoned often to his office, and that suited me just fine.

My second ask was that I didn't want to run a company whose entire purpose was to serve the needs of WeWork. I had concerns about the hyper growth of WeWork and didn't want Meetup's future to be completely based on supporting WeWork's growth. I needed to choose what was right for Meetup instead of what WeWork preferred. **Do what is right for the business.**

In hindsight, this was definitely a smart decision! The company needed to be viable as a stand-alone business. I was uninterested in a mission focused primarily in selling more WeWork seats by creating Meetup events in WeWork offices. Artie quickly agreed to both of these asks.

My third ask, the walk-away ask, was related to Meetup's founder. I really liked Scott but fundamentally believed that it wasn't possible to succeed with Scott reporting to me. I loved the idea of Scott being the chairman who would assist on key strategic projects, but Adam insisted to me that he take on an operating role. I made it clear that this wasn't going to work, and we found a compromise that Scott would take a three-month sabbatical (which he deserved more than anyone), then we would reevaluate his role, and I'd be able to make the final call on what it would be. Adam called my decision "Solomonic," and I learned that any time you received a biblical reference from Adam, it was usually good.

While these requests might sound aggressive, the best time to negotiate for anything is actually before you accept a job. If a leader does not set up the decision-making processes, reporting relationships, incentive structures, investment needs, and other key priorities prior to starting, then the leader will possibly fail before they even start. Many do. Let me underline that: Many leaders fail before they walk in their door. They are so fearful of asking for specific needs to set themselves up to succeed, perhaps because they fear the job offer will be rescinded if they seem too aggressive, that they often naively believe "it will all work out." It won't. Or they think that their compensation is the most important thing to negotiate. It's not. You need to establish what is important before day one, and how the job will be right for you. **Be pragmatic.**

Now it was time to negotiate my final compensation package. I knew I would take the job at what was offered, so instead of pretending that I wouldn't take it, I said: "Artie, I'm going to accept the job. But I can feel great about accepting the job or I can feel good about it. I don't want to pretend that I won't be accepting it. I want to feel great and I know you want me to feel great. This job is going to be hell for the next three months [Note: I was wrong. It was much longer.] and while I am going through that hell, I want to look back on it and remember that you went to bat for me with Adam Neumann and have no regrets." Even in negotiations, always **be honest**.

Artie walked out of the room. He called Adam. And Adam gave me what I asked for.

I signed the contract immediately and felt elated. I was excited to be reporting to Artie Minson whom I deeply trusted. I had drunk the Kool-Aid and believed WeWork was going to be the next Tesla and couldn't wait to get started. While I had obvious concerns, the moment I signed, they vanished. I was now focused on putting a plan in place. All I needed was a strategic plan and all would work out just as it had always worked out before. I was, of course, dead wrong.

A few takeaways from making my Decision 0: Put in the work to make the right choice:

- Interviewing is dating. Don't marry your first date, and if there are red flags during the dating process, those red flags will only become stronger during marriage.
- Be retrospective after leaving a job. If you left for specific reasons, make sure you don't go back to the same problematic situation.

- The expectations you set during the interview process will come back to haunt you. Be privately aggressive in setting goals, but better to underpromise and overdeliver.
- As a candidate, you have more agency than you may realize. If you feel like you are being taken advantage of, then point it out and say something.
- Don't miss out on pursuing a company whose mission you are aligned with. Try; if you can't succeed, fine, but always try.
- You are always negotiating and everything is negotiable.

3

YOUR FIRST THIRTY DAYS

When you accept a leadership position, the hard work doesn't start day one. It starts the moment you accept the role because you'll have an enormous amount of planning to do before you walk in the door. So your first thirty days are really ninety days compressed into thirty—perhaps even into one, your first.

I knew that on my day one, I would have 250 new employees asking me for my direction for the company. I also knew that Scott was beloved by many, and any changes I wanted to make were going to be perceived as a slight on his previous decisions. But I wasn't hired to keep things the same.

WeWork was expecting massive changes at Meetup. They didn't believe it was the right culture. They didn't believe we had the right executive team. They didn't believe in the business model, the product, the financials, or the company's growth rate. WeWork believed that nearly every single facet of Meetup's strategy and operations was wrong and massive change was required, which is why they had brought me in.

About ten minutes into my first interview with Adam Neumann, I told him, "This isn't a growth job, this is a turnaround. Unless we align on that first, we won't align on anything else." The first step in making any challenging situation work is acknowledging the problem and focusing inward. Too many companies delude themselves into believing they are in "growth mode" when they are in need of a serious fix. **Be pragmatic.**

Here is a list of ways you know you are in a very challenging situation:

- When your employees are fleeing so fast that those remaining are wondering what's wrong with them for still being there
- When every product release takes ten times as long as it should because of endless debates over priorities and features
- When you have a negative Net Promoter Score
- When many employees would rather work on the side projects that further their passions or career interests instead of those that drive company growth
- When you need to add almost 50 percent more customers each year to make up for nearly half your customer base abandoning you

Every one of the above was true for Meetup when I joined in October 2018.

I was tempted to address all these problems at once. WeWork certainly wanted me to. And I put tremendous pressure on myself to make a strong first impression. But having gone too fast earlier in my career, I learned from the resulting disasters that the old saying is true: "Go slow to go fast." Also, I was fairly sure that if I started off like a bull charging into a china shop, I would lose the respect of every Meetup employee before having the chance to earn it. Meetup had gone on a WeWork-esque hiring spree in the nine months after it was acquired by WeWork. In 2018, the company hired more than 170 people, had 13 full-time recruiters, and spent more than $1 million in search fees. The company had ballooned to 250 employees, and I needed to build as much trust as possible.

So I focused on the most immediate challenges and the key decisions I needed to make quickly. The first thirty days leading a company is like a chess opening. Your initial five or six moves will determine how the rest of your game is going to go, so you want to make sure they're the right moves.

You, in your first thirty days, will likely have to make similar decisions.

Challenge 1: How quickly do you make significant changes after starting?

I met the executive team, and as both WeWork and Scott had warned, I didn't believe they were the right leaders for the company. If I made changes too quickly, I could lose employee trust, but if I stuck with an ineffective team, the company would continue to fail.

Decision 1: Bring in top people you trust.

You need to bring in top people you trust—very quickly.

In fact, I told WeWork that I needed two people whom I trusted to start immediately. Literally, the same day as I would start. Since WeWork didn't focus on costs, they agreed. When the two people I wanted came in for interviews with Meetup's head of human resources, they were simply given offer letters instead. Not that they needed to prove themselves. I'd worked with each for three years. That's more important than a thirty-minute talk (or twenty-six additional interviews). And now that they've been with us for three years, everyone else considers them exceptional colleagues and leaders too.

In the months ahead, I would come to trust dozens of other Meetup employees, but just having those two made a tremendous difference. I've always said that if I hire an executive and they don't bring others who have worked with them in the past, then I made a mistake in the hire. Great leaders build a following of people who continue to work for them as the leader moves on. For example, when I brought in our current CTO, within three months he quickly hired three to five engineers from his network to come in and drive success at Meetup. **Be speedy.**

I next turned to the executive team. To get some perspective, I asked the WeWork leaders who'd had meaningful interactions with Meetup's leadership team about which of them were strong and which may need to be replaced. The good news was that there was a consensus. The bad news was the consensus: Of Meetup's vice presidents, only one should be kept.

As terrifying as this was to hear, I understood and respected the consensus because, as I mentioned earlier, I'd given similar feedback myself once to DoubleClick's CEO, Kevin Ryan.

The problem was, Meetup is a business that focuses deeply on building community, and Scott had created a deep, loving, and loyal community of Meetup employees who looked after and supported one another like no company I had ever been a part of. This presented a double-edged sword and was both a great quality of Meetup's culture and also an enormous challenge. To fire executives whom employees loved as their leaders would possibly put a crack in the Meetup employee community that could shatter its entire ecosystem. And the person responsible for that break in community would be me. Great way to make a first impression, huh?

The reason so many of the leaders were not the right fit requires a bit of explaining. What happens at most founder-led organizations is that the leaders a founder hires often have complementary skills to the founder. For example, if a founder is a big idea person, then that leader will often surround themselves with others who are execution-oriented. Much of the core capability of a leadership team who surrounds a founder is often about complementing the founder's strengths and challenges. When the founding leader changes, those specific attributes and capabilities are no longer valuable since the new leader often has different strengths and challenges than the founder. And that was the case with me and Scott. Scott was exceptional in certain areas of leading an organization that are weaknesses of mine (for example, communicating a long-term vision), and I am stronger than Scott in people management and operations. The people I needed on my team were simply very different than those whom Scott had in place.

A further reason for needing to change a leadership team is the psychological basis of loyalty. Leaders are nearly always most loyal to the individual who hired them and gave them the opportunity. When a new CEO is brought into an organization (like me at Meetup!), the executives will be constantly comparing their new CEO to their prior CEO in every action taken. And this is not a healthy dynamic. Actions need to be evaluated on their merit and not as a comparison. It often leads to overjudging the actions of the new leader. It also leads to a far weaker connection between the executive that was inherited and the one who was directly hired by the CEO. I knew I needed to change most, if not all, of the executive team. I also knew I couldn't fire everyone.

I sat down with Scott, the chief operating officer, and the VP of the people team prior to starting and asked each of them to rank every VP. My belief was that if there was consensus among the three of them that a few of the leaders were definitely not the right ones, it would be easier to make the change very quickly. Fortunately, there were two or three VPs who were consistently at the bottom of each of their lists and all three agreed that they would support taking swift action with those individuals.

I'd like to emphasize the importance of this approach to ranking employees. I often have found that if you ask a manager for feedback on each of their people, 20 percent will be superstars, 30 percent will be great, and the bottom 50 percent will still be considered strong and doing critical work. There is massive "grade inflation" in this approach. So, I don't do it. I will always ask a leader to force-rank their team. I'll then ask how the leader will feel if the bottom two or three people quit. Nearly always the answer is, "We'd be fine if they left." The right question is then, "So, why aren't you asking them to leave?" Forced rank is an underutilized tool in facilitating feedback about people on a leader's team and I'd encourage all leaders to use it more often. For clarity, forced rank is the simple process of ranking everyone on a team from top to bottom in terms of performance relative to expectations. The "relative to expectations" part is critical since it allows a leader to evaluate their team without being biased by an employee's level of experience. Using forced rank, before I even started, helped me make some quick decisions on leaders whom I could replace relatively quickly. Even if employees may be capable in their jobs, they may not be right for the company. **Be pragmatic.**

Within the first month, there was near unanimity that two executives were not the right leaders, and I was able to let them go. Two other leaders were able to recognize that I was likely going to meaningfully change their roles and they decided to leave, which made things much easier for me. I was also able to get two other leaders to decide to quit and leave the company. Within six months, a seventh quit and an eighth was let go. Within a year, only one leader remained in the same role as prior to my joining, the CTO. And that person, too, quit shortly thereafter. If that sounds tumultuous, it is because it was. But in the decision process, I couldn't prioritize having the wrong people on the team over employee perceptions on how I was fundamentally changing (and some would say destroying) the Meetup company culture.

Remember what Jim Collins wrote in *Good to Great*: "First who, then what." Don't focus on strategy and implementation until you have the right team. You need to focus on hiring your direct reports and in parallel gain the trust of all your employees. These two priorities are often at odds with each other, as who is going to trust a CEO who doesn't exhibit that same trust in their own inherited team?

This leads to the next key challenge: How to build employee trust.

Challenge 2: How do you quickly build employee trust, before you even start?

No one in the company knew me, and I wasn't coming from a top tech company like Facebook or Airbnb (which would have unjustifiably but inevitably given me instant credibility).

Decision 2: Hit the ground sprinting.

Scott Heiferman, Meetup's founder, played a critical role here. Many trusted him, and if he shared his enthusiasm for my hire, then by the transitive property, many would quickly trust me. A summary of what he wrote in a company-wide email:

> Big news! We found someone really good—and you'll meet him at noon ET today.
>
> Meetup needs someone right now who combines:
>
> - A very methodical approach to caring for and growing our customer and member base
>
> - An obsession for the people side: setting up teams to work better together
>
> - Experience navigating big companies to make an independent subsidiary successful
>
> That's David. When you spend time with him, it's clear how he makes companies more successful. He knows what he's not—he's not a

software engineer or UI designer. He's an organizational design/ engineering whiz with a focus on methodically growing Meetup activity and revenue. I went on a Meetup Crawl with him, he felt Meetuppy all along, and you'll sense his integrity, his heart, and his smarts.

Meetup CEO is also a really hard job, so I ask that you welcome David, hold him to the high expectations our mission deserves, have patience with him as he learns, and respect what he's here to do: David is here to make Meetup much more successful. "Change the Company" is a long-standing core value of ours because that's the way for any organism or organization to thrive, so I ask for your openness. That's one favor I ask of you.

—Heif
Co-founder & Chairman

I found this email so impressive in what it said about Scott, not me, that I've included the full email in an appendix so you can use it as a model should you have to welcome your own successor. Scott is a truly exceptional founder who has always and will always bleed Meetup red. Scott reflected an important quality of strong leadership: **Be kind.**

After the email was sent, I also prioritized taking action in building trust before I even started. I had written a series of articles about my approach to leadership and wanted to be sure employees gained an understanding of my leadership style prior to my starting. I asked Meetup's head of human resources to forward my articles to all employees after I was announced as the CEO and before I officially started. I then reached out via LinkedIn to hundreds of my new colleagues prior to joining. Many appreciated the outreach and referenced the articles as an exciting opportunity for a new leadership approach. Reaching out prior to day one enabled employees to get to know me before my start. I also asked the head of HR to organize drinks for me and all employees at the end of my first day, so I could get to know as many of them as possible. Lastly, I asked our head of HR to set up a series of "listening sessions." The key was to have no more than thirty to forty employees at each session so that, with eight sessions, I could meet all employees. By doing it in smaller groups, there would be ample opportunity for direct conversation and participation. **Be speedy.**

My previous experience being involved in many acquisitions helped here, as I approached my transition in the same way as a company that has just been acquired. I had led a strategy workstream after 1-800-Flowers.com acquired other companies. I had been a part of Q&A sessions with the CEO after Duane Reade was acquired by a private equity firm. Although I had never been a part of a new CEO transition, I decided to take the principles and lessons from the most significant change-management situations I had been a part of and apply them to my current situation—and for the most part, it worked. **Work for your employees.**

Challenge 3: How do you ensure a clear transfer of leadership, not just with the leader themselves, but with the idea of the leader: the legacy they'd baked into the company?

I appreciated how Scott addressed the transfer of power, but the question remained: What role would he play in the future, and would it hinder my ability to bring my own vision and brand of leadership to the company?

Decision 3: Respect the past but start quickly on forming your vision for the future.

"The founder's legacy" is one of the most difficult challenges a new leader faces, but you must make a clean break to establish your own legacy. Fortunately, there is a good framework for what to change later and what to change immediately. Anything that directly impacts an employee's day-to-day experience, postpone. Anything they don't care much about, do. For example, I was quick to kill or keep product features, but I took close to a year to change the company's mission statement, vision, and values.

Although I was unsure how helpful the founder would be to our company's future, I had tremendous respect for all Scott had accomplished. Meetup was, in many ways, his baby. I believed it was critical to continue to engage him in decisions to ensure that the heart and soul of the company wouldn't be lost. Every leader should try to make sincere efforts to keep the founder informed, even if only to serve the more spiritual and purpose-driven needs of a company. There is simply too much historical knowledge of critical decisions made in the past to eschew a founder. **Be kind.**

The message: Respect the past but only toward making smarter decisions and increasing the opportunity for faster organizational change. Along the way, I also learned a few best practices for CEOs who take over for their company's founder.

- *Less is more:* After a period of no growth and investor demand for action, founders often believe the answer is hiring more people so there are more opportunities for growth. After a leadership change, the staff size is often bloated, which makes it difficult to move the company faster.
- *Bring in new leadership:* I accepted my role on the condition that day one I could bring in a couple of key employees who would start on my same day. A new leader should not do this for many roles, but a couple of quick hires whom you trust can have an outsized impact.
- *Use what worked for you in your past:* While it may fail in your new role, there is nothing wrong with taking processes you trust and immediately implementing them. At Investopedia,

each executive shared with all company managers a weekly email regarding their three-by-three (three items going well and three not as well). In my first week at Meetup, we added this. If it works, lather, rinse, and repeat. There is no shame in imitation.

- *The power of quick wins:* Taking over as leader often takes a frustratingly long time to have a major impact. Find a couple of quick wins. It builds momentum and confidence. At Meetup we drove incredible early collaboration on our company strategies. It galvanized many, in a time of deep financial instability.

- *Initially err on greater consensus building:* This is a controversial recommendation, but I believe that in the first couple of months it is important to deeply listen, learn, and manage through greater consensus. The mistake I made is that I allowed that to continue for another nine months instead of moving into "directing" after my first few months at Meetup.

- *Stamp out the "we already tried that" or "we've always done it this way" mentality:* There will be many naysayers. Listen, but don't let it prevent you from acting. Learn from the mistakes of the past but be comfortable pushing back aggressively, especially if there is doubt on past leaders' ability to execute.

- *Break bad habits fast:* One of the primary jobs of a new leader is to understand a company's bad habits. Every company has them, and its employees are often too close to the habits to realize it. Identify them. Kill them. Meetup leaders often came late to meetings and had meetings with no agenda. These were bad habits and we needed to change them fast.

- *Stay close with and support your founder:* Work hard to maintain a relationship with the founder. It is often hard and sometimes impossible. But recognize that the founder is the heart and soul of your company and there are many ways they can continue to contribute. Harness that energy to drive success. It is always worth it to try.

Having worked with dozens of founders, I have found a number of consistent traits among them.

Founders tend to make decisions on intuition rather than using data. The reason is fairly obvious: They succeeded and built successful businesses initially on intuition, and it is the success from intuition-based decisions that reinforced their greater value over data. Be sure to prioritize data-driven decisions upon taking over as a new CEO.

Founders will nearly universally have pet projects and key employees whom they have nurtured and supported for years but today serve as a hindrance to the company's growth. This blind loyalty had served an important purpose for the founder. They accepted the founder for who they are and provided deep loyalty. Find them and make sure these employees or pet projects add true value to the company. You may need to remove parts of the business that the founder cherished in order to enhance company performance. **Do what's right for the business.**

Founders tend to be less organized, have an antipathy for process, and are often less focused on the commercial aspects of a company. These three tendencies serve as an enabler for the company's success in its early years but will often be a significant disenabler as the company scales. The new leader must build more processes and focus greater attention on revenue and profit, while ensuring a continued acceleration of better product and user experience.

While generalizations are incredibly dangerous to make in all aspects of life, it's incumbent upon new leaders to immediately address them since they present systemic challenges in the company's DNA that need to be ameliorated.

As per Jim Collins's advice, the "who" was dealt with, now I could deal with the "what": our strategy and implementation.

Challenge 4: How can you save a sinking ship?

Meetup was on pace to lose $20 million over the next twelve months.

Decision 4: Meet reality head-on.

Prior to starting, I asked WeWork for a copy of Meetup's financials. To say I was in shock would be an understatement. I had never seen financials that were as terrible for a company of its size. The business had no revenue growth. It had gone from breaking even to losing tens of millions of dollars. Customers were churning at an extraordinary rate. It was a mess. **Be surprised only about being surprised.**

On top of that, under WeWork, Meetup went on a massive hiring spree and was on pace to more than double its employee count from a year prior. Most companies set key metrics around improving the user experiences, growing new subscribers, and so on. One of Meetup's key metrics was actually exceeding hiring targets. WeWork literally set a goal to just hire as many people as possible and continue to grow the company's losses. *What all these employees did was secondary; let's just keep hiring people though!* Insane. The company had no marketing department but somehow had twenty employees in human resources.

Meetup was a company whose main priority seemed to be serving itself. More than $100,000 was to be spent on its upcoming holiday party, there were $4 coconut waters everywhere, they had summer parties on the rooftop every Thursday evening, and employees were able to expense items that had absolutely nothing to do with work (bike helmets, singing lessons, and the like). Clearly, if I was going to enable the company to be self-sustaining, I was likely going to need to be the grinch who stole employee fun. Lucky me. The job of a leader is to strike the right balance between what is best for the company, the company's customers, and employees. There is no right approach to the balance, but Meetup was heavily overindexed in what was best for employees and underindexed in what was needed to be done to be an effective and sustainable company.

Compounding this challenge, WeWork didn't seem to care at all about the losses—and for good reason. Who cares about a $20 million loss when the parent company is losing $3 billion? It isn't even a rounding error. WeWork only cared about finding a path to multiply Meetup's revenues a hundredfold and expected me to be the magician that figured this out. However, I had been around long enough, and made the mistake of mounting losses before, to not believe WeWork's messaging that the losses weren't important. I was confident that our losses would become extraordinarily important, and that if I didn't address them quickly, Meetup would be in serious trouble.

As a leader, it's important to know when a situation is simply unsustainable and to address that situation quickly. In my case, it wasn't a question of whether WeWork would ultimately care about Meetup's losses. I knew they would even though they swore up and down that they didn't care. It was a question of when. I also found the focus on hiring employees and driving employee fun to be a serious distraction from actually building a great product. The company was moving at a snail's pace because there were too many people to align ideas behind, too many people needed to be a part of decision-making, too many whose feelings would be hurt if they weren't first consulted. There was too much employee centricity!

As someone who started in human resources out of college, the situation was incredibly difficult. I deeply believed in employee empowerment. At Investopedia, the reason for our success was the deep motivation employees felt in building the company. I had believed that employee centricity was kind of like chocolate: You could never have too much of it.

Nonetheless, one of the most important actions a leader can do, aside from building the right executive team around them, is to ensure that the company's resources are being placed in the right areas. The percentage of people who focus on building great products and marketing those products needs to be the majority of the team. The number of "liaisoning" roles where the focus is to facilitate communication between people needs to be low. Facilitation roles are not creating value; they are often there to compensate for other people's lack of capability. Better to have people who have strong communication skills and not need liaisons at all. There were many examples of money not being spent on high ROI opportunities but rather on compensating for specific employee challenges. Other roles were created due to WeWork requests that added no value to our customers. Both needed to be fixed.

There were also enormous gaps in what the company really needed to invest behind, and I needed to kill projects and let go of people to lower total costs, grow profit, and ensure the right resource allocations by department. I knew this was going to be a long process to fix, and like any long process, the earlier we could address it, the better, and it starts on day one.

Challenge 5: What's the best way to build your initial company strategy?

I needed to build a strategy for the company quickly. Employees would be impatient and on edge until we had one. WeWork hired me to take the company in a new direction. Should I draft a quick (and likely wrong) strategy or wait until I am more informed?

Decision 5: Communicate a new direction quickly (be speedy).

I told WeWork that while my first day in the office would be October 29, 2018, I needed to "secretly start" a week prior to prepare for day one. I needed to spend an entire week meeting with our key executives to learn about the company's challenges and put a process (not a plan, but a process) together that would empower all employees to feel ownership of the company's strategy. It was more important to me that our employees feel empowered and motivated than we build the actual "right strategy." I knew that it would take a year to actually figure out the right company direction and that neither WeWork nor our employees would accept this time frame. I needed a placeholder plan to placate all parties. Hey, maybe we would get lucky and it would be right, but most likely, we wouldn't. (Note: We didn't. It was dead wrong. But it did lead us to the right strategy eighteen months later.) To do nothing would also be a decision, but it would be the wrong one.

I spent the week prior to my first day aligning with Meetup's leadership team on the most significant problems facing the company. Instead of attempting to figure out the solutions myself, I wanted to solicit the combined brainpower of all our employees. We created the following seven strategy workstreams in which eight to twelve employees focused on solving each of the following challenges:

1. Acquiring Meetup organizers
2. Engaging Meetup members
3. Driving organizer retention
4. Evaluating new business models
5. Building a Meetup brand
6. Collaborating better with Meetup
7. Focusing on fewer priorities

In my first two weeks, each workstream had a meeting every single day. Each group recommended specific solutions. Rather than me determining our strategy, I was now able to break the many "sacred cows" that existed at Meetup because our employees directly recommended them as an output of our process.

As an example, one of the workstreams asked, "We are focused on too many projects. What company areas should we kill to enable success elsewhere?" Meetup had teams of dozens of people working on projects that were going nowhere. The previous CEO was unable to shut those projects down, and it was painfully obvious to nearly every employee that it made little sense to continue spending time and energy in three areas of the company: (1) an entirely new app called Meetup Now, (2) an effort to align WeWork's office space usage with Meetup's organizer needs (the entire initial premise of the acquisition!), and (3) facilitating giant events for organizers to meet one another (which was costing the company millions). The workstream team recommended killing each of these. We had close to 20 percent of the company working on these three projects. Had I suggested it, it would have taken many months to make the decision. I would have never gained employee buy-in that quickly. However, because the "focus workstream" made these strong recommendations and presented it to the company, we made the decision relatively quickly to unravel projects that had been in existence for years. Each of the workstreams proved prescient in driving better priorities for the company in the weeks and months ahead. To this day, I continue to hear from those employees who volunteered to be part of our strategy workstreams that it was one of the best professional experiences they have had at Meetup. This process worked so well that I have repeated using strategy workstreams many more times, including to get the company out of the depths of the pandemic.

While others may have advocated for taking more time in making key strategic decisions, taking action is actually the best way to learn. We needed to learn in order to then continuously iterate on our strategy. For this reason, the sooner you can take action and learn from that action, the better.

You can't just take action in the isolation of the C-suite, though. You have to keep everyone in the company informed about what you're doing and why. Make it a priority to engage employees rather than make solo decisions. **Work for your employees.**

Challenge 6: How should you communicate tough decisions?

It's day one. I need to speak to all 250 employees, and first impressions are critical.

Decision 6: Communicate and commit to your leadership philosophy.

Focus on your leadership philosophy, not on the specifics of how you'd change the company.

I had done a tremendous amount of preparation prior to starting. I spent days with key executives, ensured the hiring of two key trusted former colleagues, planned the seven strategy workstreams, prepared for listening sessions, and organized our get-to-know-the-CEO party on day one. Now it was game time.

At 10 a.m., there was an all-hands meeting introducing me to the company. I decided that I wouldn't talk about company strategy and what I wanted Meetup to become. I didn't know that yet! Instead, I put together a list of the ten most important principles to me as a CEO. I wanted to focus more on culture building. My top ten:

10. EQ is more important than IQ
 9. Transparency
 8. Focus
 7. Revenue
 6. Performance-driven culture

5. Accountability
4. Diverse and inclusive culture
3. Analytics wins
2. Learning
1. Support and push team

Each of these principles was relevant to Meetup's future. And I would be reminding employees of them in the months and years ahead.

The only one that proved particularly controversial was #7: Revenue. Meetuppers didn't come to Meetup to grow revenue. Growing revenue was perceived as something that evil, capitalistic companies did. Meetup was all about making the world a better place. I quickly realized that Meetup had a nonprofit's mindset in putting mission first but somehow also thought that making a profit was antithetical to their mission. They didn't understand, as Art Buchwald said of Garry Trudeau, that you can sell well without selling out.

In fact, revenue is the ultimate mission enabler. I probably repeated the statement that "Revenue gives oxygen to our mission" a hundred times in my first year. Some employees were so anti-revenue that they saw my focus as unhealthy. Many others I helped to understand the criticality of revenue and that the more revenue we had, the more we could invest it into creating better customer experiences, which would result in growing our members and having a greater impact on the world.

But it was hard. Really hard. Many employees simply wanted to have fun at work and hear powerful stories about Meetup's impact on the community and were less interested in building a sustainable business model. Those employees left. In fact, employees started leaving in droves. I had never been a part of a company where so many employees were quitting. People started posting merciless reviews on Glassdoor that the new CEO cared only about revenue and profit and was destroying the company culture. I had to have seriously thick skin and be comfortable with about half the employees supporting me and the other half speaking disparagingly about me. I knew that a culture change like I was pushing wasn't going to be pretty and that there would likely be a lot of casualties. I just hoped that mine wouldn't be one of them. **Do what's right for your business.**

Interestingly, as my personal approval ratings as CEO reached a nadir, the business began to grow in revenue. First in single digits, then double digits. The company's losses, which were in the tens of millions, also began to meaningfully improve. As more employees left, those who stayed did so because they truly believed that revenue gave oxygen to our mission.

I didn't waver, I didn't compromise, and I was comfortable being an island because I had no doubt that what we were doing was important.

Leaders far more often make the wrong decision out of weakness or due to a need to capitulate to their team's desires. If a leader is sure of something, really sure, then they need to move the decision forward. Always provide the context and rationale but never be afraid of making a decision that one is absolutely confident is correct. That is what leaders are paid to do. You're not paid to manage by democracy. You're paid to decide. **Be confident.**

Overall, I made many decisions in my first thirty days. Here's the main takeaway. At the beginning, you'll be tempted to run in every direction at once. Hold back. Slow down. Focus on the most important challenges:

- Recruit new executives whom you can rely on. And who have a change management mindset. Only when you have the right team can strategy be formed and executed.
- Build trust with the employees. Take time to know them, and for them to know you.

- Lead the company according to your vision. While it is important to respect the company's traditions, you will likely have to break a few of them.
- Face the finances. If you're leading a company with unsustainable losses, you won't be a leader for long.
- Collaborate with your company's leaders to form a strategy. They will own it more, and contribute meaningful ideas.
- Strategy begins with your specific approach to company culture and your leadership philosophy. From there, you can move on to addressing specific challenges.

4

THE NEXT SIXTY DAYS

After you find your footing in your new role, you have to put your company on a better footing by spending the rest of your first ninety days dealing with those above you and below you and moving from planning to execution.

My first month was terribly stressful and far more difficult than I had expected. When I joined companies in the past, I was used to my new team embracing and instantly trusting me. Meetup was different. I was instantly distrusted. I was distrusted because WeWork hired me. I was distrusted because I wasn't coming from a top-tier tech company like Facebook or Airbnb. I was distrusted because Meetuppers tended to have a serious distrust of leaders and revenue growth more broadly.

I was struck by how employee-friendly the company was but felt it bordered on irresponsible. As someone who deeply believed in the criticality of building employee morale, empowering teams, and building careers, I was nearly always the most employee-first executive in the room. But at Meetup, I looked at the excesses and saw a culture that prioritized what was great for employees over what was great for our customers. I had never in my career seen such excesses being spent and justified as critical to driving employee morale.

It didn't fit with the incredibly strong mission of our employees, and blame shouldn't be placed on them. It was a result of all-too-inexperienced managers and leaders who believed that their primary job was to drive employee satisfaction rather than build a great product experience. I decided to call another CEO who had dealt with the same challenges, persevered, and turned around his company's culture.

Josh Silverman is the CEO of Etsy, a highly mission-driven organization that had been plagued with a deeply unhealthy corporate culture that was in part related to the prioritization of employee perks and morale over important business decisions and the customer experience. I knew this because there were numerous employees at Meetup who had worked at Etsy and vice versa. Josh agreed that Etsy had faced a similar challenge. He told me that he fixed the culture by taking two important actions: (1) Transparency: He told his team that if their motive is a higher mission, then their self-serving actions were in direct conflict with helping realize that mission. He didn't back away from it. He delivered the message honestly and directly. (2) He carefully removed employees who were creating a me-first culture that saw revenue and corporate success as antithetical to realizing a higher corporate purpose. Etsy had turned its culture around and was thriving. I believed we could do the same at Meetup.

It took a while, but nearly all companies now realize the power of having a galvanizing mission. Millennials, in particular, have become increasingly focused on working for mission-driven organizations. Due to the criticality of a lofty mission, I've seen quite a few real stretches in companies forcing a mission statement. Will a packaging organization really save the environment? Will a light-bulb company truly change our ideas of the future? But Meetup's mission and impact is real. I have personally been told by dozens of therapists that they often look to prescribe "attending Meetup events" before prescribing medication. I've heard that Meetup has saved people's lives, led to new careers and spouses, and even provided lifesaving treatment advice through Meetup's thousands of support groups. But was Meetup too mission driven? Can an organization be too mission driven?

The answer to both is yes.

Meetuppers were believers in the power of community and the deep personal growth that came from the tens of millions of users of Meetup. But there was also an entitlement and depth of employee expectations that I had never seen in my career. I didn't believe my job was to make employees happy at the expense of the company; it was to drive employee motivation as a means to driving real business results. I decided to **do what's right for the business** and prioritize company success over employee morale. It was the first time I ever needed to make that kind of decision. In the past, they were completely intertwined.

If employees distrusted me, at least they didn't despise me in the same way that Meetup employees vilified WeWork. Before I started, Meetup conducted an employee culture survey, asking employees about WeWork. I had never seen such deep loathing by an employee population for their parent company—despite WeWork indulging exactly the sort of "morale-building exercises" many enjoyed. I had heard about executive team meetings with Adam Neumann where Adam had asked a Meetup executive to down shots of tequila with him. I knew about an offsite where WeWork flew all their employees (including Meetup's) to a Fyre Festival–like summer camp in the United Kingdom for a few days where there wasn't enough food for people to eat, the porta-potties overflowed with human waste, and the company's "bro" culture proved anathema to Meetup's wonderfully diverse executive team.

So, just as I overturned the executive team by first getting rid of the most ill-fitting members, I overturned our employees' attitude by first dealing with the influence of WeWork, starting with their influence over me. Once I did these things, I could turn toward Meetup's future.

DEALING WITH WEWORK

Challenge 7: How should you work with your corporate parent?

Decision 7: Be honest about the relationship and what is realistic for success.

One of the most common fallacies in business is the concept of a merger. There is no such thing. Either you're the acquirer or the acquired. The acquirer wins and can do whatever they decide with the company that is acquired. Too often, when a *merger* is announced, it is a euphemism for "we own you." When WeWork acquired Meetup about eleven months prior to my joining, they told employees that the acquisition was a merger—but that didn't fully convey what had happened.

It has always appalled me how companies are often reluctant to tell the truth to acquired entities, saying something like "We're combining forces, but we see each other as equals. We're looking to learn as much from you as you from us. We want you to maintain your identity and special culture." They should just **be honest** and say, "We acquired you. We probably overspent in doing so. We aren't equals. We own you. You have a lot you can learn from us and we expect you to change your culture so you can be successful like we are."

That is how WeWork saw Meetup.

WeWork had spent $156 million to acquire Meetup. WeWork acquired Meetup for a few reasons:

1. WeWork wanted to differentiate its real estate offering and build real community in its buildings. And what better company to build community than the largest community platform in the world—Meetup.

2. WeWork wanted to ensure that its valuation multiple would be a "tech multiple." Meaning, WeWork wanted to justify its outsized valuation by presenting itself as a tech company—and Meetup supported that thesis.
3. Because Adam Neumann wanted to.

Let's take these in reverse order. Adam met Meetup's founder, Scott Heiferman, and the two immediately connected in the way that two founders often do. They both were deeply mission-driven. They both believed in the power of people and gathering spaces to dramatically improve the human experience. They both really wanted to make the world a better place. For all the negative sentiment written about Adam Neumann, I have full certainty that Adam believed that he was put on this earth to make the world a better place, a place where people connected to themselves and to others more deeply than they do today. Scott shared a similar belief system. Within weeks of their meeting, they were already talking about a sale.

While the negotiations were tough, the two CEOs were able to resolve key points of difference like adults. For example, upon a meaningful gap in valuation during the negotiating process, Scott and Adam decided on a unique way to finalize the price. Scott gave Adam a Meetup T-shirt to wear during Adam's upcoming trip to Israel. Scott told Adam that if he spent the day in Tel Aviv wearing a Meetup T-shirt and no Israeli commented to Adam about what a great company Meetup is, Scott would give in to Adam's demands. Now, if that isn't the way to finalize a gap in the price Adam wanted to pay compared to what Scott would take, then I don't know what is.

Scott, as it turned out, won that bet. More notable is that both sides were basing their valuations mostly on storytelling and not on true financial realities. In certain ways they both ultimately lost: WeWork due to overpayment and Meetup due to setting such high expectations on valuation that could never be justified. As noted earlier, be data-driven.

During the interview process, nearly every WeWork executive, besides Adam, informed me that they were against acquiring Meetup. So the head honcho of the company wanted it while nearly every other WeWork leader with whom I needed to collaborate believed that Meetup was a mistake to acquire. Well, if the head honcho is Adam Neumann, then he wins. Adam wanted it, and he got what he wanted.

Meetup was a Web 1.0 tech company. Everyone in Silicon Valley knew about Meetup. Hell, most of the venture capital investors had likely met founders and partners by attending Meetup events. The company had an incredibly strong brand in the tech community, and Adam wanted to ensure that WeWork was synonymous with tech. WeWork wasn't just a more stylish shared workspace with more kombucha and fewer walls. WeWork was being valued at over ten times the value of its largest competitor because it was a "tech" company. The problem, however, is that WeWork wasn't a tech company. Not at all. WeWork leased real estate and then subleased it at a high premium. Truth be told, the rationale on acquiring Meetup to gain further tech company street cred was actually quite brilliant.

But the most significant rationale for the acquisition, and one that everyone on both sides deeply believed had the greatest potential, was the fact that Meetup organizers often need to find venues to host Meetup events, and WeWork was looking for more events in its space to deepen the community bonds of its sublease tenants. The acquisition would solve a core need by each party and create a symbiotic relationship.

But it didn't work that way and here is my read on the situation based on what I saw. It was quickly apparent to both parties that the entire rationale for acquiring Meetup was incorrect. Over 80 percent of Meetup events happen during the evenings and weekends, the exact time that WeWork members aren't even in the building. Meetup couldn't provide events when their events were at a totally different time than WeWork members were using WeWork spaces. Despite the proliferation of WeWork buildings throughout the world, fewer than 20 percent of Meetup events were even in close enough proximity to a WeWork to be able to leverage its space. Finally, a meaningful percentage of Meetup events were either too large to fit in a WeWork conference room or were sport and outdoor events. Frankly, WeWork wasn't too keen on flag football around its open floor plan. Taking all these factors into account, less than 5 percent of Meetup events were at the time, location, and type to be able to leverage WeWork. The company was sold for $156 million with the premise that both companies would see meaningful synergies. (Note for nonfinancial readers: *Synergies* is a word used by companies to describe ways in which a company will grow revenue or profit through an acquisition and thereby justify a high purchase price. It's the business-speak equivalent of "we're staying together for the kids." No one ends up healthy.) Scott not only couldn't tell Adam that the premise was false, but Meetup devoted massive employee resources into projects to link WeWork's open conference rooms to Meetup organizer needs. Instead of Meetup focusing on helping 95 percent of its members, it would disproportionately aim to help this small subset as justification for the deal. So much for sunk costs.

After two months as CEO, I shut the entire effort down. It wasn't working and was being pursued only because WeWork hadn't **been pragmatic** and Meetup hadn't **been honest**. I refused to make the same mistake.

Challenge 8: What do you do when what is best for your company conflicts with the direction of your board or owner?

As CEO, should you prioritize the needs of your parent company or the needs of the company you're running?

Decision 8: Prioritize the needs of the company you are running.

A child's job is not to serve their parents. It is to become a capable, independent, and contributing human being. There is a reason why the words *organization* and *organism* have the same root; much can be learned from the other. Meetup's job was not to serve its parent company but to become a capable, independent, and contributing organization. Anything that didn't fully support this was a distraction, and making Meetup serve the needs of WeWork would prove a significant distraction. Making Meetup as successful as possible, **doing what's right for that business**, would be the best way to serve both Meetup and WeWork.

About a month after joining, I was asked to give my first presentation to the top one hundred leaders at WeWork. I tried to **be honest**. I shared my initial thoughts on the good, bad, and ugly of Meetup (which was mostly bad and ugly) and then ended with an image of a person putting an oxygen mask on themselves. I told WeWork leadership that Meetup needed to ignore WeWork requests. Meetup had too many challenges and needed to be solely focused on fixing them. Like a passenger in an airplane in deep dive due to an engine failure, Meetup needed to put its oxygen mask on first, before it could help WeWork or anyone else. The analogy worked. WeWork execs got it. From that point on, I was (mostly) given full autonomy to take care of the company's needs and not do the bidding of WeWork.

I knew my message had hit home when I got a call on my cell shortly afterward from Adam Neumann. He actually apologized for reaching out to me because he had promised he wouldn't disturb my focus on Meetup. He rarely felt reluctant when it came to involving himself in others' business, but he understood the message and, most impressively, complied.

Having established my own position, I explored how to reconcile Meetup and WeWork's very different cultures.

Challenge 9: Do you merge your company culture into your parent company's culture or keep it distinct?

Decision 9: Keep your own company culture distinct.

There have been many studies substantiating the Rule of 150 since it was most recently popularized in *The Tipping Point*, by Malcolm Gladwell. The rule posits that the maximum number of individuals in a group that someone can have a relationship with is 150. Amazon, Facebook, and most major tech companies tend to encourage their acquired businesses to maintain their own distinct cultures. When Amazon acquired Zappos, they demanded it. Not so with WeWork. WeWork preferred to push its culture and values on each of its acquired entities—which never succeeded in anything aside from creating massive tension between the organizations.

As I saw it, WeWork and Meetup were cultural opposites in every way imaginable. Where WeWork was fast, Meetup plodded. WeWork was money-focused, Meetup was mission-oriented. WeWork was shiny and new. Meetup was gray and outdated. WeWork was plastic, Meetup was authentic. I decided I didn't want to hear complaints about WeWork from employees. I didn't want to hear about the latest WeWork gossip. I didn't care, and neither, ideally, should our team. I understood why so many of our employees were deeply impacted by WeWork's culture and people practices. In fact, we had a handful of engineers who quit specifically because of them. But our focus needed to be on building a great product and not on the weekly distractions of WeWork in the news.

After my first day, I only once had any WeWork leader in our office. Despite Adam telling me he would try to visit at least monthly, he never did. Honestly, that was fine with me. I tried to keep the company totally quarantined from WeWork's shenanigans. And I would have succeeded, but the shenanigans became too eye-popping to ignore. Allegations of fraud, misogyny, and racial biases generated articles in the news and whispers in our office. While we weren't being forced to serve our WeWork masters, their reputation stank worse than the porta-potties from a company summer camp event.

Adam Neumann may have kept his word, but WeWork's policies and penchant for being in the news severely impacted Meetup. So, just as I had to navigate Meetup's founder, I also had to figure out how to navigate our owner.

Challenge 10: Should you avoid or embrace volatile leaders?

Many of us have bosses whom it is best to keep at a distance. Adam was such a boss, but he also could unilaterally fire me, and it may not be wise to ignore the CEO of my parent company.

Decision 10: Avoid. Avoid whenever possible.

Friends often ask me what Adam was like to work with, and my typical answer is "a whirlwind." Adam was more chaotic than the press had made him out to be, but also far more soulful, mission-oriented, and impact-focused than journalists gave him credit for. Adam was extraordinarily opinionated about nearly everything, but those opinions came from a deep belief that he was put on this earth to change the world.

I first met Adam back in 2013 when WeWork had a handful of buildings and an enormous dream. Michael Eisenberg, who had initially introduced me to Adam, was the largest outside investor in

Seeking Alpha, where I served as president. Michael asked Adam to speak with Seeking Alpha's board and executive team. I was mesmerized by Adam and remember thinking to myself, *That is someone I want to work for one day.* Adam either amazed or repelled in his first impression, an incredibly valuable capability in raising investor capital because you either left the meeting with money or the meeting was mercifully short.

Adam himself considered any meeting with him a high honor. For instance, a few months into my tenure, Adam asked me to join him on a private flight from New York to San Francisco that was leaving the next day. He told me that by the end of the flight we were going to finalize Meetup's strategy, and then upon arrival in San Francisco I would fly back to New York. I wasn't particularly interested in finalizing a strategy in the hours between 11 p.m. and 5 a.m. I'm more of a morning person and fairly nonfunctional, like most humans, at that time. But Adam was apparently most functional then. I expected these kinds of qualities in Adam. With him especially, I was **surprised only by being surprised**. Fortunately, I had a legitimate excuse that one of my kids had an important medical appointment that I needed to attend. I told him I couldn't go.

Adam seemed insulted and was livid. He even offered to change the time of the flight. He told me that no one turns down the opportunity to spend six straight hours one-on-one with him. He specifically said, "If Barack Obama offered to have a one-on-one flight with you, would you turn that down? People would pay hundreds of thousands of dollars to have an opportunity to fly with me." He told me that I had to join him to ensure quality time together. I refused again. It wouldn't be good for me and would potentially lead to a strategic course for Meetup that made little sense. After that experience, I went from beloved to disliked—and I actually preferred to be disliked. Flying too close to the sun can give you a terrible burn. The gain wasn't worth the pain for me.

Earlier in my career, I would have been terrified of losing the relationship. But once you have no further career aspirations than your current job, it provides the freedom to lead in the way you want to and not need to pacify others and thereby sacrifice your personal values. I had believed that Meetup would be the last corporate role I would take. There was no ambition to do anything more than to see this wonderful company succeed.

If more leaders could **be confident** enough to lead as though they had nothing to lose if let go, I believe they would perform far better. At least I know I would have been a better leader in the past if I had the confidence never to let personal ambition get in the way of smart leadership.

Challenge 11: How much should you trust your parent company or board's direction?

I needed to decide whether to trust WeWork that they didn't care about Meetup's staggering losses.

Decision 11: Be pragmatic and long-term focused.

Don't ever trust any direction that lacks financial accountability and solely prioritizes short-term imperatives. Good leaders know that when it comes to finances, one must **be pragmatic**, and when it comes to priorities, one must **be long-term focused**.

Our revenue growth goals were tricky. Adam Neumann had told me that he expected Meetup to be a $1 billion–revenue business within five years. The business took eighteen years to get to about $35 million. It had almost no growth and was now expected to more than double revenue each year. That looks pretty good on a spreadsheet. So, in what is the most inane of exercises, but a typical one that thousands of CEOs have done for millennia, we put together a five-year plan for Adam that had absolutely no basis in reality.

WeWork actually asked for two financial models: the "Adam" model and an actual model that made sense. We would send Adam his model to show how using fanciful assumptions we could hit $1 billion revenue. Many of these assumptions had about as much chance of actually happening as WeWork actually being able to fulfill its mission of elevating the world's consciousness. We then put together a more realistic model. It required strong juggling, as when we met with Adam we'd pull out the Adam model and when we met with WeWork we'd use the actual model. Adam believed something similar to what Theodor Herzl said about the founding of the State of Israel: "If you will it, it is no dream." Adam fundamentally believed—and had seen successes that reinforced this—that if you truly believe you can accomplish something, however fanciful it may be, then your dream will be achieved. The job of the CEO is therefore to dream big. While I admire that ambition, the negative consequences are enormous because it impedes realistic planning and financial forecasting, like leaping off a skyscraper and figuring you'll learn how to fly on the way down. If I couldn't **be honest** with Adam, I had to be with other WeWork executives.

In making a decision, it is easy to listen to your manager or board and take them at their word as a basis for whether or not to prioritize profit or to continue to make dramatic and unproven investments in a company. After I was hired, WeWork execs had sworn up and down that they weren't worried about Meetup's losses. I believed them, and in truth, they had no reason to be worried about the losses when they represented less than 1 percent of WeWork's far more massive losses. The difference, however, is that WeWork was experiencing dramatic revenue growth through its investments and Meetup hadn't experienced any real growth in years. In fact, the only thing growing was the company's payroll and its mounting losses.

On a personal level, I love investing in a business. When I took over as CEO of Investopedia, I took the company's profit down from about $4 million a year to $1 million a year but was able to turn that investment into tripling the companies' revenue in three years, which led to a meaningful growth in profit. After Investopedia was sold and the new parent pulled back on all investments, the company's profit was able to skyrocket to more than $10 million. But at Meetup, the company had just decided to hire enormous numbers of people, which mostly served to create an environment where no one knew exactly what to focus on, and the company's product development cycle slowed, as there were too many cooks in the kitchen. It wasn't working. To be more successful in delivering a great product to our users, I needed to reduce costs and people first and foremost. Secondarily, I was also very worried about not learning from my past (at Duane Reade and Everyday Health) and **being "surprised"** when on a dime, WeWork would inevitably change course and make profit a driving factor. In fact, when WeWork portfolio company CEOs and I would get together, we would ask ourselves not whether but how long it would take until the WeWork gravy train would end. We knew that their ignoring profit was short term, and the prevailing belief among my colleagues was to simply let it ride and enjoy the financial freedom while we had it.

I was **being pragmatic**. This financial freedom and ballooning number of employees created many roles at Meetup that were bullshit jobs. David Graeber wrote the fantastic book *Bullshit Jobs*, which contends that more than half of societal work and corporate jobs are pointless. In my experience, there are two types of jobs. Jobs in engineering, product management, customer support, sales, and marketing are doing real work. People in these roles create, sell, and market products. Other roles in finance, legal, human resources, project management, and line management are primarily focused on minimizing risk, facilitating communication between people, and helping direct and motivate their teams. While incredibly important, they aren't directly impacting the business. Kind of like the CEO. Let's **be honest**: I fall into the second category. I am overhead. In a perfectly running organization, there would be no need for a CEO or other indirect impacting roles. To quote an oft-used phrase in political campaigns, "You organize yourself out of a job." Of course you need a CEO to manage corporate friction, but a company should focus the vast majority of its resources on hiring individuals who are directly impacting the product and its users and not BS jobs. And Meetup had a tremendous number of BS roles.

BS roles are oftentimes created and tend to linger for a variety of reasons, and it is incumbent upon leaders to sniff out and stamp out those roles, for three primary reasons:

- Risk aversion: It is important for a company to minimize its downside risk by ensuring there is a legal team, people team, tech security specialists, and PR crisis managers. But companies will often hire too many personnel for these roles instead of investing in direct-growth roles. A risk-minimizer primary role is oftentimes best served by a consultant who can be brought in when needed versus as an ongoing full-time hire.
- Poor communication: The answer to a company whose leaders and managers are poor communicators is not to hire a full-time communications manager (as Meetup did) but to ensure the company has leaders who are capable of effective communications. Leaders need to check on what roles exist in an organization where the primary responsibility is to compensate for incapabilities.
- Career opportunities: Companies often have their heart in the right place and want to provide increased management opportunities to retain their top individual contributors. However, a manager of one or two people is often incredibly

inefficient (unless it is purposely being done as a path to managing more people soon or for a specific mentorship opportunity). Companies create these new roles to retain performers, but it also drives inefficient structures.

The sheer number of indirect product- or revenue-generating roles was debilitating and did not enable getting things done. People had to create work for themselves that often got in the way of others' work that had greater business impact. Regardless of the losses, to **do what was right for the business**, we needed a layoff.

But the losses were also a real issue. And I needed to learn from my past experience as a GM at Everyday Health and not make the same egregious mistake as I had made about ten years prior.

Everyday Health is the second-largest health and wellness publisher (after WebMD). I was hired to build a new revenue stream focused on connecting our thirty million users to local health care providers—physicians, hospitals, and so on. When I joined Everyday Health, I was also told that the company was in investment mode. Losses were insignificant, and I was expected to acquire companies and build a team with minimal regard to cost and maximal focus on revenue growth. Sound familiar? If so, it is because it is the story of thousands of pre-IPO tech companies who justify outsized valuations with an ambition of over 50 percent revenue growth. I built a staff from 0 to 150 employees in eighteen months. We were really starting to grow a meaningful revenue stream, and then the company decided to go public. Everything changed on a dime. I was told I needed to slash costs and make the business profitable ASAP. It was a total 180-degree turn. (Why people call it a *360-degree turn* makes no sense. If it is a 360, then you are back where you started. You're still just going in circles.) I was asked to put together a list of most of my team to let go, and I included my own name.

I wasn't going to make the same mistake at Meetup and believe that I was in a situation with no financial accountability. The reckoning for WeWork would come. It would come quickly, and I knew it would be devastating. The time to cut costs and save Meetup from this reckoning was as soon as possible. Sometimes "experience" is incredibly valuable, and this was one such time.

There were a number of challenges to making a layoff happen quickly. I had just started and it would be a great way to eliminate any trust I had built in my first month. It was already December and near the holidays, and the golden rule of HR is to never have layoffs right before a holiday. It would also present the second straight year that Meetup did a December layoff, a likely trigger for future Decembers at Meetup.

Layoffs are just completely unfair to employees. It isn't their fault that their management did a terrible job forecasting costs. Meetuppers just wanted to create a great company and they were now stuck in a situation that nearly none of them (except the executive team) created. They would suffer for leadership's poor decision-making.

Thus I was faced with my second set of critical decisions during my next sixty days in office.

DEALING WITH OUR EMPLOYEES

Challenge 12: What is your goal in a layoff—I mean . . . a reorganization?

Every decision is anchored in a goal. If you don't set the right goal, then you won't make the right decision. While this is fairly obvious, not enough time is usually spent on aligning on the goal of a key decision.

Decision 12: Make cuts needed to set you up for long-term success.

I made a serious mistake in our own goal for the layoff we were planning. But before I share the details with you, I want to share a falsehood uttered by every head of the people team related to a layoff. They always say, "Never use the word *layoff*!" I disagree. Calling it a reorganization, reduction in force, downsizing, or any of the other euphemisms attempts to cover up the harsh reality of a layoff. Don't try covering it up. **Be honest.** Pull off the Band-Aid. Call it what it is: a layoff.

My goal for the layoff was to shut down those areas of the company that were a distraction and eliminate the roles of lower-performing employees. I took a minimalist approach. My goal was not to set Meetup on a course of financial health, but only to make the most obvious changes. Of the 250 employees, we eliminated about 25 positions. We should have eliminated 100. And had we done so, we may not have needed more layoffs in the future.

I was weak and also somewhat scared. I was overly optimistic about our ability to grow revenue quickly, and we suffered the consequences of that decision for many months afterward. It is always a difficult decision to reduce costs. And oftentimes, that difficult decision results in not reducing enough costs. Do not be overly optimistic. It is better to cut more expenses than you think in order to ensure that you don't keep having to do so. There's a real fear of reducing costs. But the greater fear is that the challenging times could end up lasting significantly longer and you'd have to do something that's difficult again. The fact is, you'll never regret going too deep. If you do, you can always hire people back. I didn't, and I deeply regret that. It was the result of setting the wrong goal.

Challenge 13: How transparent should you be about an impending layoff?

Being transparent is one of the most important traits a leader must have. Transparency builds trust, and only with trust can you achieve a motivated and aligned team. Without it, either the team has to go—or you do.

Decision 13: Communicate directly to employees.

Be transparent about company challenges, but a certain amount of opacity early on will help you avoid chaos.

Usually layoffs begin with the impacted employees being suddenly called into conference rooms, which inspires whispers and private Slack channel messages, then company-wide paranoia. Employees spend all day in fear of being the next person tapped on the shoulder and asked to proceed to a conference room and returning to their desk to find their email shut off already.

Meetup's layoffs needed to be different. They needed to **be kind**. There would be no shoulder tap. We wouldn't shut everyone's emails off immediately. We were a community platform, damn it, and we needed to treat our fellow Meetuppers as a community and with the respect they deserve. We would not be the shoemaker's children who were barefoot—the community platform that killed its community.

On December 6, 2018, less than six weeks into my tenure as CEO, I called a meeting of the entire company. I explained that as a result of our strategy workstreams, we needed to shut down a significant number of initiatives. I told them that we were able to find roles for certain employees working on those projects (the superstars) but that we would be "saying goodbye" to twenty-five of our colleagues and friends. I didn't want people finding out through whispers. I wanted everyone to hear the information directly from me.

The silence was of course deafening.

I explained that within five minutes every employee would receive one of two emails. They would either be asked to meet in a conference room or would be told that they were not impacted. While these five minutes (which ended up being only two) would be terrifying, at least they would **be speedy** compared to the hours awaiting the shoulder tap. I informed employees that we wouldn't be shutting off anyone's email. We wouldn't be asking people to leave. Impacted employees could stay in the office until we had our all-hands meeting later that day and we were all there to support them. I asked employees to galvanize together to create a list of every HR and executive leader in other companies who may be looking to hire our people. We'd help every person find a job, and we were going to be overly generous in severance packages. We were going to **work for our employees**, even the ones who were leaving.

I then went back to my office and sat there, with my door open. I wanted to send a message that anyone who wanted to chat could stop by and I wasn't going to hide from people's concerns. And then the strangest thing happened.

A woman came into my office and asked if I could give her a hug. While reluctant to do so due to the importance of keeping a physical distance from people as CEO, I welcomed the hug. She said that I was doing the right thing. Her job made no sense. It was costing the company a lot of money and wasn't adding any value. Wow. That's impressive.

Five minutes later, another employee came in and told me that if she were the CEO that she would have also eliminated her own position, as the role also made little sense. She told me that she believed that Meetup was finally in the right hands since I was willing to make changes that others had feared to make even though they were painfully obvious. She told me not to worry and that I needed to ensure that Meetup was going to be a healthy business or it would have no future.

One of these women I tried to hire back to another role six months later, and I served as a reference for the other one as she decided to pursue an MBA. One of my favorite mantras is "The people know." Don't try hiding the truth. People are smart. They always know if a company is healthy or not, or if their role makes sense or doesn't make sense. The people always know and pretending otherwise is just lying to yourself.

Because you may have to lay off people yourself, I've put my speech in the appendix so you can use it as a template for your own.

But be sure to read the next decision first to see how not to answer the obvious question your remaining employees will have.

Challenge 14: How do you avoid losing the rest of the team when laying off part of it?

Decision 14: Communicate openly with employees.

As Ben Horowitz wrote, in one of my favorite leadership books, *The Hard Thing About Hard Things*, "The people who stay will care deeply about how you treat their colleagues. Many of the people whom you lay off will have closer relationships with the people who stay than you do, so treat them with the appropriate level of respect." Ensuring that our 225 remaining employees believed that we treated all those we asked to leave with respect was paramount. We gathered back together and I spent over an hour answering questions from dozens of terrified employees. I was asked why I couldn't just eliminate snacks and why I needed to eliminate positions. I was asked how we chose whom to keep. I was asked many questions and handled all fairly well. There was one question, however, that I was asked that would haunt me for the rest of my time at Meetup and continues to haunt me to this day.

I was asked if we would ever have another layoff. I was worried that our employees would live in fear of another layoff. I was worried that they would never trust me again. And without thinking twice, I said two words that would haunt me for years. I said, "We're done. There won't be any more layoffs." I kick myself every time I think about this.

Nearly every time I have made a serious HR blunder it was due to a need to be liked or to make employees feel better. It was a terrible mistake and proved to be untrue less than a year later, and employees remembered it. The pressure on me to provide comfort and a sense of finality to the remaining employees was enormous, but I should have found other ways of providing that safety without promising something that I couldn't know would be true. I never could have predicted the problems at WeWork that would ensue, but I knew that WeWork's model was unsustainable and that its stumble would be Meetup's stumble, and when all stumbled there could be another round of layoffs. I was overly optimistic and refused to believe that we would ever go through another layoff, and if we did, it would be years away. Lesson learned the hard way.

Challenge 15: How quickly should you hire your new team?

In parallel with planning layoffs, I needed to make decisions about our executive team. As mentioned earlier, I was convinced that we did not have the right executive team and knew we would be unable to succeed until I brought in new leaders. Should I hire fast, knowing I would likely make a few mistakes, or put more time and thought into hiring my new team?

Decision 15: Hire your new team as fast as possible.

I decided to **be speedy,** and hire the team as fast as possible.

When a team is unsure about who their leader will be, they feel unsafe. When individuals feel unsafe, many of them will decide to find a new opportunity. We couldn't have doubt in the new executive leader driving key talent away. I have found that it is often the fear of the unknown that is more debilitating than even the negative of the known and I needed to assuage those concerns quickly. As long as Meetuppers felt uncertainty about their leaders, we would be unable to move the business forward.

My first step in replacing the new team was to **expand my options.** I reached out to more than one hundred tech execs with whom I had worked over the last twenty years and basically said, "I'm looking for everything: tech leaders, marketing, finance, engineering, product. I need to build an entirely new executive team." I also specifically asked for female and diverse candidates. I have found that unless you truly make it a priority to ask for and source a diverse pool, your interview pool of execs will skew white and male. I had made the mistake at Investopedia of not hiring from a broader pool of candidates, and I was very careful to ensure that our leadership team would be less than 50 percent white males.

I received about fifty recommendations for individuals I should speak with and took two or three interviews a day over the next couple of months. We had our most senior internal recruiter dedicate himself solely to executive recruiting and diverse and women candidate sourcing. I have a fairly strong opinion about using search firms: never use them. I would rather get referrals from my network for top executive candidates to consider than work with a search agency to source applicants. In my twenty-year career, I've hired more than fifty VPs and probably close to a thousand employees and have never used a search firm to hire a direct report. Hiring executives is a process that

I want to be extremely hands-on with, and sourcing directly is an opportunity to learn more about a candidate. In the first few months, I was hiring executives at a record pace. It was dizzying for the current executive team, as I had them meeting with dozens of candidates. We hired three general managers, a chief marketing officer, chief financial officer, and chief product officer. Our leadership team was starting to gel and employees were excited about the quick decisions I was making and the decreasing ambiguity around future company leadership. Each of the hires worked out well except for one.

I hired Benjamin (not his real name) as a business manager. He was my second choice; my top choice turned us down. I was desperate to make a quick hire, as the team B2B business was floundering due to a four-headed leadership model that preceded me in which all four of the senior individuals in the business seemed to have equal say and nothing could get decided between any of them. We needed a single owner of the business to gain any momentum. Despite some concerns, I hired Benjamin. Within two days, I heard that he seemed to always look nervous and lacked confidence. A couple of days later, I was given a number of examples where he didn't seem to grasp some basic concepts that the team was sharing with him. After spending time with him on his one-week anniversary, I realized I had made a terrible mistake. There was absolutely no way he was going to work out. I was certain about it. He had also already "lost" most of his team's confidence in only one week. The next day I explained to him that I didn't think it would work out, and it was better to make the decision quickly than in three months or a year from now. It wasn't fair to him, but it also wasn't fair to the team or the company to keep him on ceremony. We gave Benjamin a very generous severance and let the team know that we took swift action. The team was shocked. Not that we let him go, but that we listened to their issues and were so concerned that we acted as quickly as we could. Here are some best practices to executive hiring in general and the process of building an entirely new executive team in particular:

1. Never ask for a reference: References are bullshit, as anyone can get a couple of people to speak highly of them. They mean nothing. Forget references; you need to backchannel the hell out of every key hire. Fortunately, I am fairly well connected and a quick LinkedIn search will tell me how many connections I share with someone. I then reach out to every connection and ask for feedback. Backchannel; don't get references! But don't just backchannel when you are hiring someone. Backchannel when you may join a company. I was deciding whether to accept the job as CEO of Investopedia and had heard conflicting feedback about my future managers—Barry Diller and Joey Levin, the chairman and CEO of Investopedia's parent company, IAC. I then called John Foley, someone with whom I had built a relationship when I was at 1-800-Flowers.com. John had worked with Diller and Levin for years and spoke so positively about them that it was probably the most influential reason I took the job. John then told me that if I changed my mind, he was working on a business plan for a small idea related to cycling that he was passionate about. I should have probably been discussing taking an executive role at his "small startup," Peloton, instead!

2. Hire fast: You can have someone meet with thirty people and it likely won't help you make a smarter decision. Ensure you know the two or three most critical priorities of a hire and don't look for an impossible candidate that is great at all fifteen items of import. It is impossible to find someone that checks off every box, and this will only delay your making a hire. In my experience, the number of solid hires to "Benjamin" hires is ten to one, but people take forever to hire (and spend a fortune doing so) because they're afraid of the rare Benjamins.

3. Set the new hire up for success: I would send reams of reports, documents, spreadsheets, and the like to every new executive hire and ask them to read what I shared prior to starting. Execs are expected to know a lot on day one and really hit the ground running. By pre-sharing a lot of information, you enable the new exec's success. Too often I hear from hiring managers that they don't want to overburden a new hire. In reality, you are only helping a new hire actually be *less burdened* once they start the job by sharing helpful information prior to their starting.

4. Hire for complementary skill sets: If as a CEO I am too strategic, I need to make sure that each of my direct reports skews high in execution. If I am overly analytical, I need to be sure that my direct reports are more big-picture. The same goes for the team that the leader will inherit. If the team skews too high in one area, then hire a leader that is complementary to those skills.

5. Be cognizant of the impact of each leader on the leadership team: I started to see an unhealthy divide taking place in many exec teams. There are the new execs, full of energy, bright-eyed, and often naive. Then there are the previous leaders who have "been there and done that" and see all the challenges in trying new approaches. There was an increasing distrust between the new team leaders I hired and those who had been with the company for years. And it just wasn't fair to either group. I dealt with it by talking about it head-on with each leader and as a group. It got better but we had so many leaders exiting and joining that it was impossible to have any leadership continuity until a good year after I joined.

I've shared some best practices in hiring executives, but the most important part of the hiring process is the actual interview with potential candidates. Companies are terrible at evaluating and hiring leaders. And hiring new leaders is one of the most important jobs of a CEO.

Challenge 16: How do you interview an executive?

Decision 16: Use the four-step framework.

Considering the impact of hiring the right leader, it is extraordinary how little innovation there has been over the last fifty years. Candidate sourcing is most often a referral from a trusted source, followed by a series of interviews that either evaluate a leader's fit on too many dimensions or on one specific priority (often to the detriment of others). The most common mistake I have seen in the evaluation of a leader is for an organization to swing too heavily to the opposite of the incumbent. The previous leader was too in the details. Hire a big-picture person! The previous leader was too soft? Hire a jerk!

Interviews are disorganized, open-ended, easily manipulated, and more akin to a comfortable chat at the bar than true probing on experience, capability, and vision. No data-driven approach is used and there is no coordinated effort. I've interviewed for only two CEO positions in my life, and was hired for both. More often than not, the hiring of a leader follows one of two paths:

1. Overdirecting: The most influential decision-maker (board or CEO) really likes the potential hire. The decision-maker then either actively or passively bullies the other interviewers into hiring their top choice. The most common form of this is passive bullying as opposed to active. It is also the most dangerous. The hirer makes it clear that person X is their top choice and the burden is on others to dissuade them of their perception.

2. Overempowering: The most influential decision-maker is a wimp. The decision-maker is looking for universal acceptance of the hire. Because the ten (or in my case more than twenty) individuals involved in the interview process each may have five to ten key priorities for the hire, the potential hire is someone who

becomes impossible to find. Everyone interviewing is looking for different capabilities, and hiring will take many, many months until frustration sets in and the influencer moves back to over-directing the hire.

It is rare that the right balance is struck in evaluating potential leaders. I developed a four-step framework to improve the executive interviewing and evaluation process and find the right balance:

1. Guiding: The final decision-maker should provide the three to five most critical capabilities they are looking for in a hire and explain the context of why each is important. Decision-makers should ask for any feedback on the list but ensure there is full alignment by all. If interviewers ultimately disagree, then they need to "disagree and commit."

2. Directing: Recruiting needs to direct which interviewers should be evaluating which skills as well as record any "watch-outs" that arise in the interview outside of those core areas.

3. Listening: The decision-maker needs to listen to, but need not follow, the perspectives of interviewees. Ideally, if there are red flags, then follow up directly with the candidate.

4. Time boxing: Executive hiring can unnecessarily take many, many months. It is important that there is a high sense of urgency, as typically there is significant organizational instability during the hiring process.

WeWork's hiring process for my position at Meetup was a combination of the weaknesses of both overdirecting and overempowering. Adam took an instant liking to me and I believe was the strongest voice in the room in facilitating my hiring. The company interviewed fifteen to twenty other candidates but it was more to ensure they had a broad perspective than because they were really looking for a better fit. I then had to take twenty-six different interviews since every person needed to have an opportunity to provide feedback, even though I was told that their feedback and meetings were more of a formality than they were actually valuable to the decision-making process.

How much executive interviewing is just about getting buy-in to a decision that was already made? Most of the time, interviews are used to gain buy-in to the hiring decision rather than help make a smarter decision. This isn't bad per se. Most people are ill-equipped to be able to interview and select the right candidate. If the final decision-maker is confident and just hires their top choice without feedback from others, it prevents the new hire from building critical relationships prior to starting. So, is there a better way? Yes. **Be honest** and transparent with someone interviewing a new leader that "it is likely that we'll move forward, but we want to hear if you have any red flags." I think this more open and direct approach will result in better and faster decisions.

DEALING WITH MEETUP'S FUTURE

My final priority during my first ninety days was rolling out a company strategy. I had solidified how we would work with WeWork, laid off 10 percent of the staff to drive greater focus, fired and then hired a new executive team, and now had to finalize our 2019 company strategy. The challenge I faced was similar to the one I faced regarding hiring my executive team: speed or surety?

Challenge 17: Do you install a placeholder strategy to give your organization a star to steer by, even if it is a minimum viable star; or do you develop something more informed by facts that everyone can be confident in?

Decision 17: Go with an imperfect plan over no plan at all.

We couldn't go into the year without clear objectives and we couldn't set those outside the context of a larger growth strategy. Like most of my early decisions, I decided it was better to **be speedy** and build a plan that I knew may be incorrect than to have no plan at all.

The company had done some quick work on the seven strategy workstreams (see p. 46), and in about a week (from the December 6 layoffs to mid-December) I wrote our 2019 company strategy. After the layoffs, the company desperately needed to understand what we would be prioritizing. As I was hiring executives, they needed to know what they were signing up for. WeWork also was asking me what I would be prioritizing. Again, I decided to prioritize speed, knowing we would just need to iterate and update what wasn't working in our new plan.

While Amazon is known as an incredibly difficult culture for employees, it is also performance-driven at its core and has a number of exemplary practices. My two favorite models are Amazon's virtual ban on PowerPoint presentations and their writing of press releases on major product launches. PowerPoint (or Google Slides) presentations are inefficient and one-sided. They don't drive dialogue. Amazon asks their teams to create a document and have the document be read in the first five to ten minutes of a meeting. The rest of the meeting can then be spent on thoughtful debate and disagreement and talking *among* people rather than one person *at* people. The second practice is one I employed when writing Meetup's strategy document. Amazon asks its product managers and other leaders to create a press release of what would be written if a new product or business succeeded. I decided to **be bold**, borrowing that practice and publishing a fictitious article as an introduction to our strategy about Meetup's turnaround coinciding with the company's thirty-year anniversary.

Here's what I wrote:

December 2032: Meetup Celebrates Its Thirtieth Anniversary

In Jan. 2032, *The New York Times*, in partnership with the World Health Organization, released its "Life Well Lived" obituary competition, the latest advancement from their data-generated journalism team. Subscribers were told to simply upload their deceased relative's Lifestream CV—a verified record of the person's life, family history, and genetic records—and an algorithm would appraise that life's potential. The computer scored how well one's potential was fulfilled on a scale of 1 to 100, providing an objective evaluation of whether it was a "Life Well Lived," and noting what could have been done to achieve greater fulfillment. Readership surged. The *Times* highlighted the highest-scoring "Life Well Lived" each week, but what readers gravitated toward were the obituaries with the lowest scores—the ones showing the extent to which people had destroyed their potential by spending time on pointless interactions.

Then something curious happened. Lifestream CVs uploaded for living people began to rise, outpacing those uploaded for the dead by ten to one. Everyone wanted to know what their "Life Well Lived" score was and how they could improve it.

A year later, the editors published an analysis on what actually comprised a life well lived. They interviewed thousands of readers who had achieved a high score and asked what their secret was. The vast majority cited Meetup, the leader in real-life experiences that had achieved enormous success (to the tune of a $10 billion valuation) over several decades. Meetup, they said, had empowered them to confidently pursue a life well lived by rejecting one dominated by digital distractions. Ninety percent of members reported an increase in their sense of connection to others, and 95 percent of organizers reported an increase in confidence and leadership skills. They had intentionally immersed themselves in meaningful relationships and real-life experiences, which have been on the decline since Facebook launched in 2004.

David Siegel, the fifty-eight-year-old, long-standing CEO of Meetup, shared why the company may have played such a significant role in these "Lives Well Lived." "We always dream big as a company, and we set goals to ensure that we are actually helping people pursue their full potential," he said. "Meetup members have always known that the best way to achieve personal growth is through real, human connections."

After this forward-looking vision, I enumerated the company's one-, three-, and five-year objectives, key results, and financial targets. WeWork loved it, employees were galvanized by it, and it set a direction for what bets we wanted to make and where we wanted to pull resources. It wasn't loved because it was particularly thoughtful or well written. It was loved because it put a specific stake in the ground and could drive direction for the company.

Looking at it over two years later, there was so much that was wrong about the strategy we had decided to focus on. But I don't see that as a failure. We needed to put a plan out there and knew we would find the right priorities only by making decisions and evaluating the opportunities I had initially documented. Sometimes you get lucky and the initial strategy is exactly right, but that is almost never the case. The initial strategy needs to be written in order to learn about what the right approach should be, and it may take one, two, or even three or more years until a company gets there. This isn't a failure, but it is the result of being honest about what is working and being willing to iterate quickly on what isn't. And aside from relying on luck, it is the best way I know how to run a company.

It is also why I am so put off by "strategic" people. A colleague of mine who is a partner in a major venture capital fund asks every hire, "Are you more of a strategy or execution person?" If anyone says "strategy," they are out. Great strategy is actually quick execution and iteration. It is setting hypotheses and conducting tests to confirm or disprove those hypotheses. It is executed against a set of assumptions. That is real strategy work—not what you put in a document and parade around as the company savior.

Most employees don't understand the criticality of having an iterative strategy. They often perceive a leader who iterates on strategy as someone who is unable to make up their mind. It has often required incredible amounts of my energy to help more junior employees in particular understand that strategy is about learning. It is about using the lean startup approach of building a product, measuring what is working, and then learning about what to do differently. Strategy isn't about what is written on a piece of paper; it is about the tests you conduct and updating goals accordingly.

Meetup's strategy was **long-term focused**, changing its business model over time to add two new sources of revenue and significantly decrease its dependency on its current revenue source. I believed that the company's core revenue source of subscriptions from organizers was significantly hampering the company's growth. Organizers are the lifeblood of Meetup. They create all of our amazing groups and events and build strong followings—and these very organizers also pay Meetup for the privilege of doing most of the work. I believed that instead of organizers paying Meetup, we should pay our organizers. We should enable being a Meetup organizer to become a full-time profession.

By paying organizers instead of getting paid by them, we could multiply the number of organizers on our platform tenfold. I felt that at that point we were like Uber, asking our drivers to pay us for the privilege of driving. It didn't make sense to me. Instead of our current revenue source, we would drive company revenue by focusing on two other sources. Members would pay a very small fee to attend Meetup events and companies would increasingly look to sponsor Meetup groups and events. Member revenue and corporate revenue had the potential to far exceed our organizer revenue over time.

We rolled out many experiments and built an entirely new business based on these assumptions. We made a lot of mistakes and have learned much, but suffice it to say, many of these growth ideas were proven incorrect. More on this later.

The honeymoon was over, and after ninety days I was already feeling burnt out. I was waking up in the middle of every night worried about the endless decisions I had to make every day. I was used to my four years at Investopedia where from day one we were able to immediately grow revenue. Over my time at Investopedia, revenue grew every month for thirty straight months. I went from feeling as though I was the greatest CEO on the planet then to questioning if I might be the worst CEO now.

Of course, neither extreme is true. Naturally, humans and organizations have an instinct to go to extremes, to say, "Wow, we're killing it, now we're unbeatable," and then to find out later how beatable they actually are. Or they think, *We have challenges and there's no hope for the future*, when in reality that approach will result in there being no solution ever being realized. Remember that it is never as bad and never as good as one thinks. But I was working incredibly hard to get Meetup to be a thriving company. It isn't fun running a flailing company like the one I had taken over, and I was impatient to have the fun of being part of a big-growth company again. Had I known that two years later (though mostly due to the pandemic) the company would be healthy, but hardly thriving, I likely would have just given up after these ninety days. I had inherited so many cultural, technical, product, customer, and other challenges that it was truly naive of me to believe that I'd turn the company's business around in a mere ninety days. While it is good to be ambitious, it isn't healthy for yourself or your team to have the unrealistic expectations for a quick turnaround that I had set.

At the same time, had I said, "We'll be OK, but it is going to take two years or more for us to get there," no one would have signed up for two-plus years of challenges. This is where optimism and transparency can either conflict or be critically complementary. You need to be honest about your concerns for the business but confident that you and your team will find the path to greatness.

In sum, then, the next sixty days require you to move from planning to execution. This is a tall task. Here are the key steps to do so:

- Tell your board or corporate parent the most pressing problems with your company. It's hard to resolve these problems without first aligning with your board first.
- Prioritize the needs of the company over the needs of your owner. Both will ultimately benefit.
- Keep your company culture distinct. If your company has been acquired, you don't have to adopt the culture of the acquirer.
- Sacrifice personal ambition for smart leadership. I sacrificed my relationship with my good-hearted, but volatile, boss to ensure I could run the company with the right strategy. You may have to make a similar sacrifice. It's worth it.
- Be financially accountable. Even if you are free to operate at a loss, ensure your losses are justified by a clear later return.
- Lay off the right number of people, not too few. Neglecting this difficult task dooms you to repeat it.
- Be transparent about layoffs. Employees will fear the process less and respect you more.

- Hire executives quickly. Best practices include the following: backchannelling references; looking for skills that complement your own; considering the candidate's impact on the rest of your executive team; and not waiting for the perfect person. Once you've chosen your new executive, help them prepare for their role, even before they start.
- Use interviews to evaluate the candidate's skills. I rely on a four-part framework: (1) guide the interview to focus on the skills you are seeking; (2) direct interviewers to evaluate the candidate according to those skills; (3) listen to the interviewee's perspectives, but you don't need to follow them; and (4) time-box the interview process so it doesn't last forever.
- Pick an imperfect plan over no plan. You will perfect your plan later through trial and error.

5

THE NEXT NINETY DAYS

Leaders are often given a grace period for their first ninety days (and for some fortunate CEOs their first one hundred days) during which anything that goes wrong is fully blamed on previous management. And in point of fact, this is justified. There is oftentimes almost nothing leaders can do in their first few months that will have a meaningful impact on growing revenue or building a great user experience. I have seen some leaders continue to blame previous management for years afterward, and while this may be justified, it never serves the leader well.

After the honeymoon is over, though, it's time to build and make the decisions that will lead to better products, revenue streams, a strong corporate culture, and a path to profit.

During my personal second quarter at Meetup, I was less in desperation mode to build a team and fix our finances, but I still needed to decide on several critical issues, starting with how we could become a real company.

Challenge 18: When and how should your company become "real"?

A company that doesn't have a clear path to profitability and is fully supported by investors or its parent company is a fake company. Why? Because if the investors or parent company changes its mind, then the company would cease to exist.

A company that doesn't provide any meaningful product differentiation relative to competitors is a fake company because even if it has had historic success in sales or marketing, its advantage is not sustainable.

A company that does not have the proper controls, processes, and reporting in place to ensure appropriate feedback loops and smart decisions is a fake company because it cannot maintain its health without the right strategic and financial processes.

Meetup was a fake company. (Ironically, WeWork, given its dependence on SoftBank and seven [!] series of investment, was just as fake.) And fake companies run the risk of dying quickly. Meetup's mission and impact on millions of people was too important, however, to have the company fail, so we needed to turn the company into a real company. That meant a path to profit, a differentiated product, and the right controls and processes to ensure smart decision-making moving forward.

Decision 18: Set short-term goals that lead to long-term strategy execution and iterate.

Many people think that CEOs, due to their position of power, have tremendous abilities to control and deeply influence every aspect of a company. That is both true and not true. Here's my take: Bad CEOs exert that deep influence and good ones don't. A good CEO realizes that their job is to hire the right people and build an organization's capability to make smart decisions. A bad CEO often doesn't realize how little influence they should have on certain decisions and pushes forward, only to micromanage, disenable, and ultimately force the exit of good people, whose responsibility it should have been to make those decisions. In other words, a good CEO delegates power and **works for their employees**, while a bad one clings to power and makes their employees work for them.

The decisions that you should prioritize are these:

1. *Determining who is on your executive team.* This is significant and must be done thoughtfully. Don't worry about your executives' own teams, though. While you can influence their hires (by recommending candidates, taking part in the interview process, and dismissing candidates for cause), you can't be the owner of these hires. Your executives need to own and, therefore, be fully accountable for them if someone fails.

2. *Setting a broad strategic direction for the company.* Determining the strategy is critical. You also are the final decision-maker on the key company objectives. You are not, however, the decision-maker on the specific goals and key results within those objectives, and you certainly aren't the decision-maker on the specific tactics for how those objectives can best be achieved. Tell your people what you want them to achieve. Trust them to figure out how to achieve it.

3. *Establishing the strategic, financial, and management processes that guide decision-making.* This one is a big deal and an area that most CEOs pay less attention to than they should. As a CEO you make few actual decisions, but you can ensure that there is the right framework, timelines, checks, and balances to ensure that the right decisions ultimately get made. If you're having to make too many decisions, that's a sign that these things are out of whack.

I had focused primarily on the first and second priorities in my first ninety days, but I lacked a critical partner in building financial and management processes—namely, a CFO. Unsurprisingly, given the company's dismal financial situation, Meetup didn't have one.

Meetup had finalized its 2018 objectives mostly through conversations between Scott and Adam. Trouble was, the objectives were nonsensical, the result of Adam telling Meetup's management team what their objectives needed to be. That resulted in the company pursuing projects and priorities that not only didn't move the company forward, but had little to no buy-in by the actual doers in the organization. Hell, most of the management team didn't even believe in the objectives. The result: Meetup wildly missed nearly every one of its annual objectives, and Scott was asked to leave.

Adam Neumann also believed that objectives should ideally be massive stretch goals, a philosophy shared by many entrepreneurs. The idea is that the harder you push people and the more visionary the goal you set, the greater the likelihood you will achieve that goal. You won't achieve it otherwise. WeWork set insane goals and that was one of the many reasons for its meteoric rise.

I, however, have a different philosophy. Prioritize small wins and iterative planning. After establishing long-term plans, teams need to set quarterly goals that are achievable and sustainable. This allows leaders to create quick wins, build confidence, stoke employee morale, and then reset goals each quarter based on the current state of the business. The iterative nature of the goals is more important than their aggressiveness.

Because the future is so unpredictable, having a visionary plan is not enough. Planning must be accompanied by a thorough process to iterate. Never just set it and forget it. The magic is in putting together a series of hypotheses that may or may not be proven true, which then influence the ultimate plan. Then, continually evaluate whether or not you have the right plan and be nimble to shift the plan as needed.

It took me a few months to find the CFO I wanted. She and I then went to work overhauling nearly every process in the company. We built frameworks for weekly, monthly, and quarterly financial reporting. We overhauled our goal setting and review processes by installing monthly check-ins and quarterly reviews. We created daily, weekly, and monthly dashboards to track each of the top priorities because if you don't inspect it, you shouldn't expect it (as I learned from a

Duane Reade executive who visited at least one store every day for many years). To be long-term focused, especially on profitability, we needed short- and medium-term goals.

It was great to have someone who had truly deep domain experience in her field. She knew exactly what she needed to do, and I trusted her to do it. We also prioritized finding a path to profitability by moving resources in our customer-support and engineering organizations to lower-cost locations. At Everyday Health, Seeking Alpha, and Investopedia, a meaningful percentage of our team was either outside of one of the United States' most expensive hiring markets, New York City, or outside the United States entirely. Meetup, on the other hand, was paying in some cases 500 percent more for a customer service rep in the United States than one in the Philippines and more than double the fully loaded cost of an engineer in New York City versus one in Ukraine.

I had no interest in outsourcing the entire organization. Ideally, you want a blend of here and there. For us that meant balancing in-house engineers and customer support with the ability to scale and drive greater profit through independently contracted engineers and customer service representatives from lower-cost countries. Given that I'd inherited more than one hundred engineers and forty customer service reps in New York, this was obviously not a popular vision.

Like the layoffs, I took a wimpier approach than I should have. Instead of **being bold**, and making significant changes, I decided we would slowly wean ourselves away from high-cost employees to low-cost employees and contractors and replaced each higher-cost NYC-based employee with lower-cost resources. Events, including our sale out of WeWork, later forced Meetup to make more dramatic reductions in head count in high-cost locations.

Ultimately, these changes to Meetup's workforce definitely worked. In two years, we went from 100 percent of engineers and customer service in New York or Berlin to about 40 percent of our engineers and

15 percent of our customer service team in New York. This one action, more than anything else, let us increase our 2019 to 2020 profit from a loss of $18.5 million to a gain of more than $3 million.

We focused on moving the company from a fake company to a real company, which meant one word: sustainability. My goal was to ensure that Meetup would always exist no matter what, even if a pandemic hit the company and virtually wiped out in-person events. But that would never happen!

Challenge 19: How to address company culture

During my second quarter, I also had to rebuild the company culture to fit the next stage of Meetup's development. This is never an easy task, and its difficulty is probably why most new leaders let a lousy culture continue to fester after they arrive. So start small by first asking yourself the two questions I did: What is the goal, generally speaking, of a company culture? What goal are you specifically looking to achieve?

Decision 19: Decide on your core values with full engagement of employees.

Broadly speaking, the goal of a company culture is to (1) build sustainable employee behaviors that (2) provide an advantage (3) relative to its competitors. Most employees perceive the goal of a company culture as creating a fun work environment for employees. In fact, culture is so often equated with a "great employee experience" that the very term is often synonymous with why an employee may choose to leave: "Our culture used to be awesome, but now we are cutting back on costs and the fun is gone." Before explaining the culture I wanted to build at Meetup, it's important to parse these elements of culture.

Build sustainable employee behaviors: A culture represents a company's DNA. It represents the habits of a company. Those habits aren't one-off behaviors, but consistent and sustainable behaviors that could be incredibly healthy or unhealthy.

Provide an advantage: This advantage could be helping recruit or retain top talent and focusing on impact to employees. A culture also has a significant impact on a company's customers. There is no right decision on culture, but being mindful of whether you are building a culture that is about competition or teamwork, about strategy or execution, about focusing on sales or on product, is important. Each of these cultural trade-offs will have a significant impact on the company's strategy and ability to build a great company—and goes outside of solely impacting a company's employees.

Relative to competitors: Whether the culture helps a company attract top talent or the culture is highly client-centric, it provides a sustainable advantage or disadvantage for a company relative to its competitive set.

So, in answering what culture I wanted at Meetup and then how to build that culture, it really came down to what employee behaviors I was looking to build to provide a deep competitive advantage and how to ensure that those behaviors would be sustainable. It came down to **doing what's right for the business**.

After an acquisition, many companies talk about the challenges of *tech debt*. Namely, that for years, a company took a short-term approach and never invested in a long-term technology to drive success. But companies rarely talk about *culture debt*. While Meetup had terrible tech debt, I also inherited culture debt. The culture was one that completely lacked any financial discipline. It too often prioritized the interests of employees over customers, and it had both a fear of failure and an inability to make data-driven decisions. It was a real mess.

A culture results from the priorities and capabilities of a company's founder and the previous management team. So I believed that by changing the company's management, we would be able to quickly overhaul the culture. I was wrong, again.

Our leaders tried to get the company to focus more on revenue and financial discipline. We tried to build a strong process around making data-driven decisions. We looked to take big bets. But we were often stymied. We were never held back due to intentional efforts to hurt the company. We were held back because our directors, managers, and employees had been acting in a specific behavior pattern for many, many years and those habits were incredibly hard to break. It seemed like no matter how often we explained that there would be no negative impact to setting an aggressive goal and missing it, employees feared setting ambitious goals. No matter how often we explained the criticality of data-driven decisions, employees made decisions by gut when analysis could have provided a better direction.

It actually seemed like we needed to overhaul a majority of our managers and leaders across the company in order to build the culture we needed and that no amount of mentoring and training would have the desired impact. And that's pretty much what it took. Little by little, managers left or were asked to leave, and we were incredibly intentional about the behaviors we wanted in their replacements. We needed to hire leaders who were optimistic because for too long, Meetup managers' pessimism resulted in their teams' low morale. We needed to hire managers who had real experience explaining the context and rationale for decisions because we had too many managers who believed that their sole responsibility was to support their teams' needs and not provide context for corporate decisions.

A few things we tried did work. For instance, I brought back the strategy workstream process that had been so helpful earlier, and we created a new workstream to focus on drafting the company's mission, vision, and values.

The company had been using the slogan "Meetups for everyone, everywhere," which provided absolutely no focus. After significant work, iteration, and employee buy-in, we evolved it to "Empowering personal growth through real human connections."

The company also had two sets of values with some broad similarities but no details that were in common. One was created by Scott, our founder. It consisted of nine values with three subvalues each, for a mind-numbing twenty-seven attributes. No one could remember any of them. The other was created by the head of the people team and used for recruiting. That list consisted of the eight values the company was most looking for in new employees. After dozens of employee meetings and a high level of engagement across the company, we aligned on six values that represented what Meetuppers most stand for. There were so many employees involved in the effort that we barely needed to roll it out since nearly everyone had seen versions of it throughout its development. A tremendous amount of time was spent on this—and it was worth it.

It's important to remember that you almost never want to "roll out" something so core to a company as its mission or values. They should be developed through such a deeply engaging and evolving process that employees are there through each step in the process. You want employees to feel invested in the values, not imposed upon. Today, we use our values in recruiting, our performance management reviews, our 360-degree development feedback, our employee surveys—you name it, we use them. I speak about them with every new employee, and they are values that help direct whom we hire, fire, and promote. After creating the values, we had each Meetup employee place a tag at their workspace listing which value most resonated for them. It is the anchor in how all key decisions are made, and we expect employees to raise their hand and say, "We can't do this; this is against one of our values."

They haven't changed since we rolled them out. They are **long-term focused**. Here they are:

TRUST in TRANSPARENCY
Access to information allows us to debate, align, and act. Collaboration thrives in clarity. Because we know transparency builds trust and trust is the foundation to open communication.

FOCUS on IMPACT
Smart decisions start with prioritization. Forward motion depends on taking risks. Because we know progress requires boldness mixed with strategy.

INVITE CHANGE
Adaptability opens the door to opportunity. A willingness to welcome the unknown is essential for innovation. Because we know change transforms everyone's future.

STEP UP
Accountability begins with ourselves and ends with each other. Ownership includes knowing when to offer and when to ask for help. Because we know we all have a responsibility in doing whatever it takes to achieve our mission.

ELEVATE PEOPLE
Our success is collective and relies on bringing our whole selves to the conversation. Assuming the best in one another reflects our commitment to celebrating our differences. Because we know human connection depends on showing up for each other.

LEAD with INTEGRITY
Our actions carry weight, which is why ours are rooted in respect. Doing good work is more than just doing a good job; it's doing the right thing. Because we know having values means nothing unless you live by them.

I also wanted to build a culture that really partnered with our managers and directors in making collaborative decisions. I often find that the leadership teams make too many decisions in isolation, without working directly with managers and gaining their important perspectives and buy-in to decisions. I set a monthly meeting for me and all directors and another one for me with all managers. That evolved into a weekly meeting of all managers. We give them a heads-up on company strategies, we ask for their help and input, and I reserve a section of each meeting for extremely open and transparent Q&A where anyone can ask the most confidential of questions. It is often better to make slightly worse decisions that have full manager engagement and buy-in than to make the "right call" and have others misaligned. In decision-making, manager input and buy-in are critical. And a culture where managers will disagree but fully commit to a direction, even if they don't agree, is equally essential to business success.

I also made a few missteps in building our culture. I wanted to drive a more revenue-oriented culture and believed that if we created a rallying cry that this nomenclature would drive behavior. I started talking incessantly about "$42.2 million" (our revenue target). But no one had any idea why we chose this number, whether it was the right target, or what would happen if we missed the target. It completely fell flat. Fortunately, there were enough employees who told me that it wasn't working and I was just confusing people with such a deep focus on a specific target. It was a good lesson that real change can come only through deep, integrated communications like our mission-setting process, and not through superficial slogans.

Another failure was my looking to add a Ping-Pong table to our office. I asked our office experience team to buy the table. We did, and immediately a few women let me know that they felt uncomfortable being in an environment with a Ping-Pong table, which they considered the ultimate "bro tech company game." I had absolutely no idea. I asked a few of them what we should do, and a couple of the women told me we should get a foosball table that would be played by people of all genders. I quickly agreed, only to be told by a couple of other women that foosball was also too male. I mentioned that I got the foosball table only because two women had suggested it, but that didn't matter. This was an area that I really felt ill-equipped to navigate, and I quickly realized that I should probably avoid any activities that could discomfort anyone. Not an easy task, but critically important. To build a better culture, I needed to **be confident** enough to make mistakes and learn from them.

Challenge 20: Should you empower those you don't fully trust or micromanage them and possibly demotivate them?

Having worked with Meetup's employees to rebuild the company culture, I now had to tackle our leadership culture, which is distinct. Ours empowered employees to the extreme, which is good in theory, and which I believed in, but in our case wasn't driving the results we needed. Thus, another dilemma. (Note: When you're a leader, its dilemmas all the way down.)

Decision 20: If empowering is not working, it's time to micromanage.

To tackle this one, I needed to change the way I always believed leaders should lead and do the opposite of what I had always taught others (and wrote earlier). I needed to throw away the axioms in every management book I had read. Success at Meetup would come only from me being overly directive. I would try not to be a big jerk. But I would **be bold**.

Prior to joining Meetup, I had a leadership formula for what I believed would guarantee a successful outcome. Much like Hillel's dictum, I simply needed to treat my employees the way I wanted to be treated. I had always hated (and still hate) to be micromanaged, so I simply needed to create a successful environment for our employees in order to get the most out of them. As the psychologist Frederick Herzberg said, "It's the job of the manager not to light the fire of motivation, but to create an environment to let each person's personal spark of motivation blaze." Empowerment was my calling card. I deeply believed in the concept of the "one-minute manager," whereby one's goal as a manager was to make oneself nearly obsolete.

The logic was incontrovertible. If you encourage an employee to make their decisions (instead of directing them), they will be far more motivated, work harder to prove their decision to be the correct one, and be fully accountable if it is not. Empowering employees pushes the decision-making down to whomever is closest to the user problem and therefore in the best position to make the decision. Empowering employees also maximizes their learning and creates meaningful organizational capability to continue to learn from and make smarter decisions in the months and years ahead.

I believed that empowering was like chocolate, always good and sometimes great. However, much like nearly everything else at Meetup, I had to significantly modify my entire management philosophy. I spent my first year empowering leaders and teams. And it wasn't working. I needed to take the reins.

"Prioritize this specific project."

"This is the skill set you most need on your team."

"Our company policy needs to change ASAP because the current one is not working."

I started to become the opposite of the leader I had always been, getting deep in the weeds on so many decisions I never would have been involved in at other companies. I would have hated to work for me. But the approach worked. I was getting in the weeds on a myriad of decisions that as a CEO I would have never been involved in previously.

It became important to ask myself why directing decisions was working so well instead of empowering others to make them, and whether or not being directive was sustainable. In self-reflecting, here were some of the reasons:

1. *Culture of fear:* I had inherited a culture where employees and teams were so concerned about making a mistake that they would

analyze, debate, and discuss decisions for months before making them. By directing, we acted faster.

2. *Lack of experienced teams:* Too many individuals had been promoted into roles in which they lacked experience. That resulted in their oftentimes simply making the wrong decision when empowered to do so. Instead of relying on knowing what works and replicating that, all too often teams relied on their gut, which was not sufficiently experienced.

3. *Unfocused teams:* By empowering teams, we had eight different product teams all working on eight different problems in eight different ways, none of which were supporting one another. Empowerment had resulted in silo work that became incredibly inefficient.

4. *Lack of a sense of urgency:* Teams feared deadlines. They believed that a deadline was an artificial date that did more harm than good to a project due to rushing to hit a date. Deadlines were perceived as dangerous. The result of this was that we couldn't effectively plan anything since we never knew how long something would take and when it would go live.

5. *Low morale:* As empowered teams worked on projects, they increasingly became frustrated because the project would take too long to launch. Managers often lacked the skills to complete it effectively, due to poor planning, and they often changed course halfway or never launched anything at all. Empowering was actually leading to far more confusion, lower morale, and employee attrition.

6. *Misaligned incentives:* Too many employees were prioritizing projects on topics they either wanted to learn more about or for which they had a personal passion. Those projects were not helping drive the key metrics of the company. They were mostly helping the individual to build their skills.

A year later, when the pandemic hit, I decided not to empower teams to figure out what to do. I told them we must create an online event experience as soon as possible because the company's entire future was at risk. When I started seeing managers hiring people whom I knew were the wrong hires, I spoke directly with managers and with recruiting on exactly how we needed to change our hiring process. I was aware that what I was doing wasn't sustainable, but the alternative of continuously failing wasn't either. I told my management team (whom I now trusted) that I needed each of them to be far more directive than they had ever been, even if it was beyond their comfort level. Some executives were able to make that transition and others who were unable to do so were asked to leave. We needed our leaders to tell their teams the what, the why, and even often the how. We needed to go against every management book we had ever read and direct, not empower. We needed to set strict owners, timelines, and clear frameworks to quickly make and then execute decisions.

While I mentioned a number of cultural challenges that made directing more important than empowering, there was really one primary reason for the importance of directing decisions at Meetup (or any company in a similar situation). Our challenge was that we had simply too many potential projects that could significantly improve our company. With literally thousands of potential actions we could take to optimize certain screens, experiences, and customer flows, on the member, organizer, consumer, or business side, it became critical to prioritize top-down exactly what to work on. Companies with too many options are often at a greater disadvantage than companies with too few options. David Packard, the founder of HP, famously said, "More organizations die of indigestion than starvation." At Investopedia, I had to do two things: grow website visits and grow the value of each visit. That was it. It was straightforward, measurable, and therefore momentum building. Meetup suffered from the paradox of choice and suffered indigestion from having too many growth opportunities. As David Packard had warned, we were unable to effectively select the right priorities and risked organizational death.

When individuals or organizations are given too many choices, they face inertia and often not only fail to make the right decision, but fail to make any decision at all. So I made the decision to be far more directive with my team. I still believed in empowerment, but it would take time for us to return to this approach.

Challenge 21: Implementing your growth strategy

The third key decision I made in my second quarter as CEO was implementing our growth strategy.

Should you choose one tactic and focus on that, or sprinkle resources around a myriad of tactics in the hope that one of them bears fruit?

Decision 21: Align with your core values and focus on the few opportunities that will really drive success.

Focusing on impact couldn't just be a value on Meetup's wall. We needed to live it.

It is often too dangerous for a new CEO to choose only one growth tactic and put everything behind it. It is also equally dangerous to choose seven opportunities and put one-seventh of the resources in each.

In this case, I let our values guide us, specifically our desire to *focus on impact* and *embrace change*. An important heuristic for leaders is to determine a company's core values first, ensure alignment on those, and then focus on company strategy and business objectives. Too often, companies will build a strategy without first documenting the basis for decision-making: a company's values. We aligned on our values quickly and were now able to **be confident** enough to make some critical decisions to ensure we were focused on fewer opportunities and putting all resources toward those.

So I shut down a business that was focused on building an entirely new Meetup App that had no plan for revenue.

I shut down sales for a business that was unable to close new clients but that kept throwing more money and resources at a problem that would be solved by neither.

I shut down a business focused on doing enormous brand building for in-person events that was costing the company more than $3 million a year with no discernable return.

I shut down our pedestrian focus on international growth, with the belief that our results in English-speaking countries were so challenged that we needed to focus here first before we attempted to grow in non-English-speaking countries.

I shut down our Berlin engineering office, as costs for salaries plus travel became even more expensive than the cost of New York City engineers.

Instead we focused on one single priority: building a better business model that could accelerate our growth. My initial research on Meetup had led me to believe that asking organizers to pay for Meetup stunted the growth of the company and that the most value was being provided to our members, who rarely paid for that value. As I brought new executives into the company, I shared my perception of an opportunity for a better business model and nearly every new executive enthusiastically supported this thesis. We then dug deeper into our data and realized that when members did pay a small RSVP fee, the likelihood of them showing up to the event nearly doubled. Coincidentally, our organizers' top complaint had been around members who RSVP'd but did not show up to the event. The change would benefit all parties. We then ran a financial analysis that showed that our company revenues would actually double if we were able to capture a $2 RSVP fee in lieu of an organizer subscription fee. Sounded like a real win for nearly all constituencies. Business success doesn't need to be a zero-sum game. There are elegant solutions where all parties—our members, organizers, Meetup, and our employees (the quadfecta!)—can win, and it is a leader's job to find every one of these and not assume that all decisions present binary outcomes.

In this new business model, I envisioned a world where our organizers, who are the heart and soul of Meetup, would be able to get paid as opposed to paying to organize a Meetup group. By enabling organizers to be paid, it would significantly increase the number of potential meetup group organizers. The "gig economy" has been a decades-long trend and more individuals, and especially millennials, were eschewing work for traditional companies in hopes of having the flexible schedule and meaningful ownership that comes with being an entrepreneur. Many people don't wake up one morning and say, "I want to pay to become a community organizer," but hundreds of millions of people are interested in becoming entrepreneurs. They want a space to **expand their options**. A wine lover in Scotland could use Meetup to create classes and a following (he did). A mountain climber in Iceland could use Meetup to build a hiking business (she did), and millions of people around the world could do the same.

The company supported these moves because we were deeply engaged in our values, and our values supported this strategic shift. Building the right anchor for decision-making is critical to driving alignment. Our anchors were our values.

It now became increasingly easier to provide the context and rationale for making decisions—it was because our decisions were a direct result of our values. If we needed to decide whether to open our financials up to the entire company, it was our value of *Trust in Transparency* that provided an obvious answer to the question. If we needed to decide whether to invest in manager training, again, we looked at our value to *Elevate People* and the answer was obvious again. I felt the company starting to build momentum.

Ninety days in, the company's problems are often perceived (unjustifiably!) as your fault, not the previous leader's. Here's how you address them:

- Set short-term goals to achieve your long-term strategy. Small wins boost employee morale and permit for iterative planning.
- Form company culture with engagement from all levels of employees. Real change can come only from deep and frequent communication about change.
- If empowering employees doesn't work, you may be forced to micromanage them. While it is better to empower employees, sometimes that simply doesn't work.
- Your growth strategy should concentrate on the few, strongest opportunities. Companies fail more often by lacking focus than by focusing on the wrong opportunity.

6

THEN THE UNEXPECTED HAPPENS

In your third and fourth quarters as leader—second semester of your freshman year, as it were—things get real as the consequences of your earlier decisions start to play out. This can be exhilarating—and depressing—and that's before everything goes sideways. It's also the first time that you should be held accountable for the decisions made in the first six months on the job. It's likely you made a few mistakes. Which is good. If you didn't, then either you haven't learned about the mistakes yet or you took the easy way out and didn't make any meaningful decisions.

Challenge 22: What to do when employees are leaving in large numbers

Me, I had to watch a parade of Meetuppers leave the company, and they couldn't have been more excited to do so. I had never seen anything like it. Nearly every week there were multiple goodbye parties and drinks after work. It seemed as if we were celebrating people who were leaving more than we celebrated anything positive we were doing.

It was easy to see their leaving as a lack of confidence in me as a leader. And it hurt.

If you were in this position, how would you staunch the bleeding?

Decision 22: Let them go and start rebuilding.

First, some background on why the parade of exits was so painful. When I was CEO of Investopedia, we had received every recognition related to employee satisfaction. We won *Fortune*'s Best Company to Work For. We were on *Crain's* list of the 100 Best Places to Work in New York City. We won the Business Intelligence Group's Best Publisher to Work For—for three years straight! We had one of the highest employee retention rates of any tech company I had ever worked for, with less than a 10 percent employee turnover rate, as compared to an industry average of about 30 percent.

Glassdoor is a platform that allows current and former employees to provide anonymous feedback on the company and its leader. CEOs often look at their Glassdoor ratings to gauge employee sentiment. One word: Don't! It is perhaps worse than a CEO who is obsessed with their company's day-to-day stock movements as a gauge of performance.

Meetup's Glassdoor ratings were plummeting, and I believed it would start to prove difficult to hire top talent as word was getting out that everyone worth anything was leaving Meetup.

On top of that, nearly everything that had caused success at Investopedia was driving either failure or marginal results at Meetup. Ben Horowitz, in *The Hard Thing About Hard Things*, provides a phenomenal overview of whether to base decisions on being in "wartime" or "peacetime" mode. In one manager meeting, I asked all managers to read that chapter of the book, and I asked whether we were in wartime or peacetime. And the response was nearly unanimous: We were in "wartime" mode. Massive change was needed. I had to **be bold** and significantly change my leadership approach to one that I was less comfortable with, in order for Meetup to succeed.

This taught me an incredibly important lesson about leadership: A successful leader can't expect to lead one company in the same way they led a prior business. Our team needed to take many of the opposite approaches to management we had taken in the past, starting with our approach to employee retention.

So, after significant soul-searching, I realized that employees deciding to leave wasn't actually bad. After another month, I shifted even further and began to embrace—and significantly thank—each employee who decided that Meetup was not for them.

Each person who left was essentially saying, "This is no longer the culture for me. I liked the big parties or the ability to work on dozens of different projects or a community of mission-passionate colleagues, but things have changed and I want to move on." Some weren't interested in building a sustainable business, while others were deeply interested in doing so but no longer had the confidence we could achieve it. And I didn't want people on the team who didn't have confidence in our future. Whatever the reasons people left, it was far better for individuals to leave and for us to replace them with others who didn't have the experiences that made those incredibly talented individuals hardened and dubious about Meetup's future. It is a perfect example of our cultural debt. In fact, I often said that had we been able to hire the person who was now leaving Meetup without the baggage that came from their years at Meetup, many would have been great hires.

This fit with an approach I'd developed years earlier called a "transparent separation." With transparent separations, you don't blindside an underperforming employee or fire them outright. Instead, you must **be kind**. Have a conversation with them. Encourage them to leave on their own by letting them know they are going to be let go in time and need to start looking for a new job ASAP.

Employees inevitably thanked me for relieving them of any ambiguity, for making it easier to find a new job because they still had their current one, and for helping them preserve their dignity and reputation. My relationship with these employees actually improved, I found it easier to hire their replacements, the company avoided legal risk, and our other employees weren't blindsided themselves by a colleague disappearing or, to use HubSpot's grotesque term, "graduating." In this case, I didn't even need to have the conversation.

In addition, each person who left was one fewer person we would need to let go if WeWork decided we needed to become profitable more quickly.

Each employee who left was doing Meetup a favor by erasing the company's "culture debt," that is, the legacy of years of unhealthy practices and attitudes. Gone were the naysayers. Gone were those individuals who made simple decisions far more complicated or managers who believed their only role was to support their teams and not to drive the company's success. Gone were those who felt that it would offend their colleagues if they made decisions contrary to their teammates' opinions.

So I didn't staunch the bleeding. I called for more leeches. We ended up replacing fewer than half of the employees who left because I was confident that our day of reckoning would come from WeWork, and as the bloated roster of 250 shrank day by day, I became more confident that each person who left us was bringing us one step closer to becoming a "real" company.

These exits were understandably very challenging to employee morale. We ran an employee survey, and it was devastating. Due to our culture of transparency, I decided to publicly share the results with all employees.

- Forty-seven percent of Meetuppers believed that Meetup was a great place to work.
- Thirty-eight percent had confidence in Meetup's leadership team.
- Thirty-four percent believed that Meetup teams collaborate effectively to get their jobs done.

Team motivation was at a nadir, and I decided to get up in front of the company and **be honest** about the many exits. It made no sense not to acknowledge them. As I previously mentioned, "the people always know." Managers often delude themselves into believing that if something isn't discussed, then it somehow magically doesn't exist. A manager's inability to acknowledge it only serves to weaken the leader instead. Always acknowledge the bad. It's uncomfortable, but not as bad.

We slowly gained positive momentum after a long period of exits. We **worked for our employees**. We brought back positive parties (instead of exit parties), by alternating a Meetup Eatup (community lunch) one week with a Meetup Treatup the next. We also returned to having summer BBQs on the roof most Thursday evenings. But it was an incredibly odd situation. I needed to motivate our team, and I also wanted more employees to continue to leave. I needed to keep our best people, but our best people were the ones who would most easily find another job.

I offered a few of our most critical employees retention bonuses, and that helped. I had one-on-one meetings with others, emphasizing how much I wanted them to still stay, but I also found that the job market was so hot that once an employee made the decision to leave, it was inevitable that they would find a great role elsewhere. We would be left with the diehards. We would be left with those people who truly and deeply believed in our mission and wanted to see it through to the end.

And that was perfectly fine by me. We wanted the diehards, and they did stay.

In fact, I decided that if people were willing to stay through all the craziness at WeWork and its derivative impact on Meetup, then we really wanted them here. The market was a perfect market. The right ones to stay would stay, and those who were the right ones to leave would leave. Because there was little I could actually do about the office, I decided to focus on how Meetup worked beyond it. That is, I went on the road.

I spoke at conferences, I met with dozens of Meetup organizers, I traveled to different cities, and I asked every Meetup organizer in each to join me for an event or drinks. I wanted to understand their goals. I made it a personal goal to go to an in-person Meetup event every week. Rather than choosing them based on my interests, I asked my assistant to book me at randomized selections of Meetup events throughout Manhattan and Westchester County. I went to a salsa-dancing event and had the time of my life. I went to a business strategy event and heard from an entrepreneur how she built her business. I went on hiking events and yoga classes, and I absolutely loved it.

My favorite part: After the event, I would speak with the organizer and only at the end let them know that I was the CEO and thank them profusely for all their hard work. I learned about what they cared about and why they had been disappointed with the product. It was awesome.

What I learned most, however, was that I should have been doing this since day one. I'd misread my initial challenge. I shouldn't have spent so much time focusing on the people side (which is really hard for a former human resources manager like me), and I needed to focus a hell of a lot more on our product and not just delegate that task to others.

I had seen so many problems internally that I felt, to **do what was right for the business**, I needed to fix them first. In reality, I would be able to do a far better job building the company strategy and ascertaining our product priorities if I spent more time talking with our members and organizers. It became one of my favorite times at Meetup. I was no longer frustrated by our challenges. I became excited about the possibilities.

Meanwhile, it was now the summer of 2019 and WeWork was in a frenzy about its imminent IPO.

The company was at its zenith. In late July, WeWork's top two hundred executives gathered at the Marriott hotel in Brooklyn for a two-day WeWork event. The focus was to tell us that the IPO road-show was going far better than anyone had imagined. They made themselves out to be Cinderella in a ballroom full of princes. Adam Neumann, followed by a parade of company executives, board members, and analysts, told us that WeWork's valuation, which had previously been $47 billion, would likely end up significantly higher once we were public. The top investment banks were talking about up to 50 to 100 percent higher. We were poised to go public in a couple of months, and every one of us was going to be at least a millionaire (and the founders, billionaires). There was literally not one negative hint of what was to come. No one shared any concerns from the analysts. Apparently, investors were jumping over each other for the privilege of investing, and banks were offering unprecedented deals to be the lead WeWork IPO banker.

On a personal level, my gut and mind were at war. My mind was swept up with the enthusiasm of all the WeWork executives surrounding me. Whether it was personal ambition for a lottery-like payout or having given into the persuasive powers of Adam Neumann and backed by the integrity of his right-hand man, Artie Minson, I believed nearly everything we were being told. My gut, however, presented a conflicting perspective. My gut was **pragmatic**. My gut had seen this before, going all the way back to the halcyon late-'90s internet days at DoubleClick. My gut had seen time and time again companies who were swept up with enthusiasm all but vanish quickly. While my mind dominated my personal decisions, fortunately my more risk-averse gut dominated the decisions I needed to make as CEO of Meetup. I would be optimistic for myself but realistic that all could still go to hell for WeWork. Meetup's need to continue to ensure independence and financial stability outside of WeWork would still stay paramount. I needed to **expand Meetup's options**, just in case.

Then the clock struck twelve; the WeWork chariot turned into a pumpkin, and its executive team turned into mice. I had never seen anything like it. It was as if every journalist, analyst, and business leader was afraid of being the first person to say that Cinderella was really a fake, but the moment it was said, it became a pile-on. Articles in the *New York Times*, the *Wall Street Journal*, and every other reputable publisher detailed Adam's behavior from pot smoking on company planes to questionable selling of assets that drove millions of dollars into Adam's personal wealth. The press was brutal.

I spoke with a number of financial journalists whom I knew from my Investopedia days and learned the truth. Journalists were deeply incentivized to write as much negative press about WeWork as they could. Negative press drove eyeballs, and eyeballs drove revenue and a journalist's reputation. Journalists would tell me that the sheer mention of WeWork in an article nearly guaranteed it to get hundreds of thousands and potentially millions of views. The more that journalists wrote about WeWork and its wayward founder, the more voracious the public became to learn more. While many journalists no doubt believed deeply in the importance of uncovering the truth about WeWork, many others simply looked to profit financially or in reputation by taking a swing to further destroy a company that was flailing for its life.

Taking down a well-known company was deeply satisfying to publishers, tech companies, and the public. The Meetup executive team and our employees watched helplessly as WeWork's valuation went in free fall, going from $47 billion (its latest round) to $40 billion to $30 billion to $20 billion in just weeks. We then started hearing that

WeWork's valuation was down to about $10 billion, and then poof, the IPO was canceled. WeWork's primary investor, SoftBank, and WeWork's board were ousting Adam. Meetuppers, nearly all of whom owned WeWork stock options, were experiencing mixed emotions: enjoying the demise of a parent company whom they mostly loathed but feeling rattled about their lost personal fortunes and worried about the potential impact on Meetup.

The shine of summer was now over, both literally and figuratively. As the weather started to turn with our ever-precarious fortunes, I decided to seek solace in visiting my father's gravesite. Since my father's passing in 2013, my mother and I have visited my father's gravesite at the Beth David Cemetery in Long Island, New York, before Rosh Hashanah each year. On September 20, 2019, while standing there, I received a call from Dan Teran, my new manager, that would determine the main focus of the next six months of my life.

Meetup was going to be put up for sale.

Already emotional at the cemetery, I was overcome with fear, uncertainty, and serious concern both for myself and our company. I had been with WeWork for eleven months, and it already felt like eleven years. After this roller-coaster ride, I yearned for stability. I asked when the planned sale would be made public. Dan told me it wouldn't be for another couple of weeks and that I shouldn't worry about the news leaking out.

A few days passed, and true to my manager's word, all was quiet on the WeWork front. Five days later, though, Dan called to tell me that he had been tipped off that an article announcing that Meetup was up for sale was about to come out in a major publication—in a matter of minutes! My first thought was, *Well, that WeWork roller coaster didn't take long to start rolling again.* Second thought: *I can't have all our employees learn about this through texts from their friends.*

Challenge 23: When do you tell the kids?

Decision 23: Immediately

Behavioral psychologists refer to status quo bias as the preference of most individuals to maintain the status quo. It is the reason that the majority of students will sit in the same seat that they chose on day one, since that initial seat is now the status quo. This bias is a result of the endowment effect, where people endow greater value to their current situation than is warranted. Status quo bias often leads to inertia in decision-making. In other words, leaders don't decide anything.

In my career, I've had the opportunity to meet with a number of management luminaries who have taught me this important lesson. The first is John Sculley, the Apple CEO who took over for Steve Jobs and was later replaced by him when Jobs returned. Prior to Apple, he ran PepsiCo and is considered a marketing genius. When I was in business school and interviewing for one of his portfolio companies, I asked him, "What made you such a successful leader?" His answer: "Anytime I have something to do, I do it immediately." That was it. **Be speedy.** I often see CEOs and other leaders afraid to make a decision, yet they seldom realize that the act of not making a decision is a decision in itself.

When I was CEO of Investopedia, I found myself sitting next to the late, great Jack Welch at a board dinner. Jack Welch was on the board of Investopedia's parent company, IAC. I asked him, "You were *Fortune* magazine's manager of the twentieth century. Insane. What made you such an effective leader?" He responded, "The most important thing you can do is to build employee trust, and the best way to do that is through transparency." Words to live by. And with the WeWork announcement, I had a chance to act on those words both in my professional and personal life.

I've also made the mistake of not acting boldly and with speed in my career and missed out on an opportunity that would have been worth over $100 million in equity today. On December 16, 2011 (I still have the email!), I received the following note from Bruce Brown, the managing partner at a search firm retained by a tiny San Francisco startup called Uber. "David, I know several folks in my organization have reached out in the past . . . I've been asked by the board to go back at you on the GM for Uber in NYC. Bill Gurley @ Benchmark insists on talking to you on an exploratory/confidential basis." Uber was looking for a head of their next city and a start of their enormous expansion. I asked my lifelong mentor, David Rosenblatt, what I should do. His response: "Benchmark and Bill Gurley are tier 1 investors and great people. Bill is high on Uber, but I don't know anything about them . . . If you end up meeting the Uber people, it is less interesting." I didn't follow up fast and with much interest and let the opportunity of a lifetime slip away. When my kids ask me how I let being an early key employee at Uber and the fortune that would have come with it slip away, I usually remark that "Uber may not have been as successful if I joined, so I didn't actually lose anything."

A final example from my personal life: Back in 1999 when my wife and I were engaged, Zillow didn't exist. Neither did Trulia, Redfin, or any other digital way to find a home. Newlywed couples looked for apartments to rent through agents or ads in the newspaper. My wife and I knew that if we went through the standard path to buying our first apartment, we'd be in competition with the thousands of others who wanted to rent. So we needed to find a more creative, proactive path than others. We spent the Sunday before our wedding walking around the neighborhood in Riverdale, New York, knocking on the doors of building superintendents in hopes of finding apartments that were not yet on the market. But that was proving inefficient since very few buildings had recent openings in the last couple of days.

We needed to get lucky by finding out about a move, right then and there. While formulating a game plan, we noticed a moving truck a few blocks ahead. We started running, then sprinting, to follow the moving truck to wherever it would stop. We then surreptitiously followed the movers into the apartment, and learned that the apartment was vacating immediately due to an emergency. We knocked on the super's door and told him we could take it that day.

Since that time, my wife and I have bought or rented four other homes. In not a single instance was the apartment or house up for rent or purchase. We proactively identified homes in neighborhoods we wanted to move to and have left dozens of notes under people's doors asking them if they were looking or knew someone else who was looking to sell their homes. My wife would take our two-year-old daughter on "day trips" to drop off notes and knock on doors of dozens of homes at a time. And guess what? Every time we have "gotten lucky" and been told that someone was close to putting their home on the market but wanted to chat with us first to see if they could avoid a real estate agent.

We acted immediately in those situations, and it was time to act immediately now, with Meetup employees.

To avoid breaching the trust I had built with my employees, I opted to **be honest**, as transparent as possible, and tell our employees everything I knew about the sale, which at the time was . . . nothing. Even though there were no definitive answers I could provide, I did know that I needed to get to them before the press did.

I told my manager, Dan Teran, to come to our office immediately for an emergency meeting. I didn't know anything, but at least I knew that Dan knew more than I did, and by having him present it would show that we were all in this cloud of uncertainty together. Misery may love company, but uncertainty dotes on it.

I sent an urgent Slack message to all employees to come down to our all-hands conference room. Dan had told me we likely had fifteen to twenty minutes until the article would come out. Employees started filing in. Maybe ten minutes left. What if Dan was wrong and we had only ten minutes, not twenty? Would I really lose the respect of our employees due to a measly ten minutes? Dan arrived. Five minutes left. I blurted out the words as quickly as possible: "WeWork is putting us up for sale!" One woman in the back screamed with joy. Literally, less than a minute later, I heard the buzzing of nearly every cell phone in the room as the article on WeWork selling Meetup came out. Disaster averted.

You don't have to meet every challenge immediately, but it's important to understand that time undermines luck. A friend of mine, for instance, frequently bemoans how unlucky he is when buying homes. For some reason others always sweep out from nowhere and buy homes he is "right about" to bid on. That same friend also seems to always come in as the second-best candidate when applying for a job. But it isn't a coincidence. He isn't unlucky. He simply deliberates too long and lets too much time pass, and that time results in him losing out on opportunities time and time again.

The CEOs of the other companies that WeWork divested didn't immediately gather all employees. They waited, and all their employees learned about their future by reading the news at the same time as their friends and family. One of the CEOs of a company also listed to be sold told me how much he regretted not quickly acting and trying to get his team together first. If WeWork employees felt vulnerable during the collapse, the employees of the handful of WeWork-owned businesses felt even more extraneous to WeWork's future, especially since every one of WeWork's portfolio companies was losing money, and cash had become king even more than it was before. By acting fast, we got lucky. It was the first of many times we would continue to engineer our luck.

Luck is rarely given the attention it deserves in driving smart leadership decisions. People are both vilified and lauded for their luck.

Luck can be used derisively or as the ultimate compliment. Successful individuals humbly attribute their successes to luck while the downtrodden blame their failures on bad luck. As the adage goes, "Hard work puts you where good luck can find you." If you work hard and smart, you can create far greater likelihoods of luck. But can you put yourself in a position to consistently be lucky? Can you take very specific actions to significantly increase the chances you will end up being lucky? Can luck be reverse engineered?

Throughout my life, my friends and family have often been amazed at how lucky I have been. Frankly, I'm often surprised about how easily most life situations have been and how well they often work out. I believe myself to be less intelligent, work less hard, and be less planful than many individuals who are often struggling in their lives and careers. In many ways, my life was quite average until I discovered the path to making luck happen at a far greater frequency than normal.

I've always believed that life is a numbers game. **Expand your options.** If you meet enough people, you will find your life partner. If you go on enough interviews, you will find the job that accelerates your career. And don't forget to **be kind**. If you try to help as many people as you can, it isn't karma that helps you when you need it most, it is the litany of people who appreciate all you have done for them who enthusiastically want to return the favor.

Luck is the result of constantly putting yourself in a situation to "end up being lucky." While the press likes to write about the lottery winner who had never bought a lottery ticket, more than 90 percent of lottery winners are regular lottery-ticket buyers. In fact, if you buy ten times the number of tickets, you have precisely ten times the greater chance of being the "lucky winner." It is your job to stack the chances in your favor by making decisions that increase the number of "lottery tickets" you can play in life.

We each make thousands of daily decisions, from the mundane (*How much cereal should I put in my bowl this morning?*) to the critical

(*Should I break up with my boyfriend of three years?*). Every decision we make will either increase or decrease the number of options of being lucky. Some decisions (but very few) are "trap doors" and decrease the number of options you have to be lucky. One of the least-prioritized elements of decision-making is whether that decision increases or decreases your available options.

Let's take a few examples:

1. Jane loves finance. But she can't decide whether to take her job offer to be a commodities trader or to work as an investment banker. She asks friends and family, and they ask her where her passions lie. She chooses trading and therefore makes an enormous mistake.

   Jane is just starting her career. There is no way for her to know what she will love until she starts her job. Being a commodities trader is a niche profession that sets her up to become . . . a commodities trader at another firm. If Jane chose to become an investment banker, she can parlay that skill into working in dozens of future professions. One decision severely limits her options and therefore her opportunity to be lucky while the other creates hundreds of potential opportunities for future employment.

2. Sam loves to paint and decides to spend the $50,000 he received in his inheritance to buy a painting studio. Sara, meanwhile, decides to invest her $50,000 in buying an RV so she can take her canvases and paints with her as she spends the next year driving around national parks, visiting art galleries, and meeting art dealers.

   Both are investing the money behind their passions, but Sam limits his opportunity for inspiration and relationship-building while Sara is creating a situation in which she can paint thousands of varied landscapes and share them with hundreds of individuals. One creates options and the other limits options. Which of the two do you think will end up "being lucky"?

Another important way that I have learned how to create luck is to ensure that all those around you know as much information as you do, so that anyone can potentially stumble upon the right decision. That leads to the next direct challenge.

Challenge 24: How honest should you be about your company's deep challenges?

Decision 24: Honesty is the best policy.

Tear off the Band-Aid. **Be honest.** Tell the truth, however ugly, and tell it quickly. Employees and customers will thank you. In fact, they might already have known the truth and will be reassured by your indicating that you're aware of it, too, and are willing to address it.

As each Meetup employee thanked me for being transparent and for telling them in advance of the news going public, I was reminded just how critical it is to ensure that employees always learn about what will impact them in a controlled environment. As silly as it may seem, the two minutes I was able to get to employees before the announcement of the sale really did make a difference.

Then, a few weeks later, in October 2019, as WeWork spiraled into disarray, I would have another opportunity to decide whether to be transparent and how much to share.

There was zero chance of Meetup not having significant layoffs after it was acquired, and every employee knew this deep down as well. Meetup employees knew that the IPO was canceled, that Adam Neumann was fired, and that the new co-CEOs had just announced in a company-wide meeting that there would be significant layoffs at WeWork. At one of our monthly employee-listening sessions, an employee asked me if WeWork's announcement that there would be significant layoffs applied to Meetup as well. I was expecting the question and waited for it. I knew we needed to tell employees, but I didn't want employees to have to go through the trauma of another emergency all-hands meeting either. This would sadly be Meetup's third straight December with significant layoffs. Terrible.

I decided that I would be as transparent as possible. I believed it was more humane to be transparent. I told them that we would have significant layoffs as well. To my surprise, there was a sigh of relief. Employees wanted to know the truth. There were already rampant rumors, and my informing employees of planned layoffs resulted in a full understanding of the situation.

Once I made the announcement, the anxiety shifted from whether there would be layoffs to when and how much. I saw employees crowded in corners whispering. Large groups of employees were going on walks together. We were in the middle of an intense process of putting Meetup up for sale, and we had a nearly complete standstill in our employees' work. We needed to make decisions and execute a plan within forty-eight hours. It was the most humane thing we could do.

Unfortunately again, "humane" and "WeWork" became a paradox. Our employees' anxiety and paranoia was at a crescendo, and the psychological toll was moving many to inertia. Meetup desperately needed to **be speedy** and move forward by completing its layoffs. But WeWork wouldn't let us.

WeWork had announced to the company that there would be layoffs but hadn't yet executed them and wanted all layoffs to be coordinated at the same time. I'm still not entirely sure whether that was a calculated decision or a product of disorganization. By holding off on layoffs, WeWork saved tens of millions of dollars in severance payments from employees who quickly quit instead of waiting for a termination. I wasn't interested, however, in saving cash but in ending the anxiety for our employees. I begged and pleaded with WeWork to allow Meetup to execute our terminations prior to their timeline. They wouldn't relent. I asked again a few days later even more aggressively. Again, they wouldn't move. I couldn't walk around the Meetup office without feeling the stress of every employee, and I couldn't take it any longer. It was probably the most difficult time I had ever had at any company in my life. I considered just not showing up to the office until WeWork would allow us to have our terminations.

I then became **bold**. I raised the level of my red alert and refused to back down. I called WeWork's chief financial officer, head of the people team, and head of mergers and acquisitions. I explained that we wouldn't be able to move quickly on the sale if employees were constantly terrified. Potential acquisition targets would be talking to our employees and would see fear, not confidence. I made the argument that it was in WeWork's best interest, not Meetup employees' interest per se, to approve the layoffs. That finally worked. We were given approval on a Friday, I spent the weekend working with our VP of people and with our leadership team, and we terminated employees immediately after the weekend. There was no reason to wait for WeWork to change their minds. Again, time was not on our side. When's the best time to take action? Immediately.

Nine months earlier, I had wrongly tried to be accepted by employees by eliminating too few positions. This time I would **be long-term focused** so we would never need to lay off people again. We decided to restructure our engineering and product teams and eliminate 75 of the now 210 employees. We would get down to 135 employees, which would put us in a position to break even for the next year. It hit the press, which didn't make WeWork happy, but I didn't care. Meetuppers were finally relieved and it was the right thing to do.

Of course, the clash between the future I'd planned for Meetup and the one thrust upon us begged the obvious question about my own future:

Challenge 25: What to do when your company is on the block

Decision 25: First try to see the big picture.

Complicating matters was the fact that WeWork's mergers and acquisitions (M&A) team told me that they wanted to sell Meetup in a month. A month! For those less familiar with a company transaction process, a typical sale process from decision to execution is most often nine to twelve months or more. It took them three months just to hire me.

WeWork believed that their goal of a one-month sales process could best be accomplished if I brought in a buyer whom I knew personally. The buyer would know me and trust me; they would know the company and, for that reason, be able to act very quickly. Artie Minson, the president of WeWork, the man most responsible for hiring me and someone whom I deeply respected, told me that I should reach out to any investors I knew ASAP and see if they were interested in acquiring Meetup.

I said I would, but I had little hope of being successful. I have never been a true startup founder, and I didn't believe I had any strong venture capital or private equity contacts. I was perfectly happy to be the corporate CEO who fully supported the WeWork sale process and "sell myself" and Meetup to whomever WeWork chose as our buyers. My identity was tied to the identity of Meetup, and jettisoning Meetup meant leaving a part of who I am. I didn't want to leave and I would follow whoever bought us from WeWork. Many leaders often feel the same and stay longer at the company they founded or lead because their personal identity is fully tied to that of the company. And this is incredibly dangerous.

In thinking about my new role in supporting WeWork's sales process, it wasn't that I lacked the confidence to try to find a buyer myself;

it was that I simply had no direct experience in ever selling a company. I placed one call to the CEO of IAC (they were the owners of Investopedia, my previous company). I told the CEO that IAC could acquire Meetup and that speed was the priority. And I got a speedy and immediate response. They weren't interested.

OK, I had made some effort, I was quickly rejected, and that was that. My paycheck came from WeWork; WeWork owned Meetup; my focus should be on supporting WeWork's M&A team and not on trying to find a deal myself. Best for me to keep my head down and avoid the fate of thousands of my WeWork colleagues who were quickly being fired. I also thought it could be seen as a sign of revolt to find a buyer, despite the CFO's recommendation. My new manager had already been terminated along with nearly every other executive who had a meaningful connection to Adam Neumann.

I knew WeWork would need more than a month. None other than Adam Neumann, perhaps the king of "moving too fast," told me that one of the most important things he'd learned was that you needed to go slow in order to go fast later. He was right. By trying to go fast, it took far longer for WeWork to sell Meetup than the company had expected.

This gave me time to reorient my thinking about my role at Meetup and not fear the unknown.

Challenge 26: Do you have the guts to go rogue and risk being dispensed with quickly?

Decision 26: Go big or go home.

A crisis presents an opportunity. **Be confident. Be Bold.**

When I accepted the role at Meetup, one of the selling points for me was that WeWork had acquired a half dozen other businesses and would be acquiring many more. I could **expand my options**.

There would be an opportunity to build relationships with CEOs of WeWork portfolio businesses in the same way that I did at IAC. Little could I know that one such relationship would transform the future of Meetup.

About a week after the announcement of Meetup's sale, I received a call from Seth Besmertnik, the CEO of Conductor. WeWork had acquired Conductor about a year prior, and Seth and I had bonded over a shared bafflement at WeWork's people practices and a deep belief in taking care of our teams. Seth is a born entrepreneur but with the emotional intelligence and people-focused sensibilities of a veteran business executive. I looked up to him not only for his business success, but also for his leadership style, vulnerability, and never-give-up approach. About a week after the sale, Seth called me and said, "David, you need to stop thinking like a CEO and start thinking like a founder." I had no idea what he was talking about. I am a CEO. I have never been a founder. And what exactly was the difference between them except my perception that non-founder CEOs always seemed to be saner than founder CEOs?

He was the first of at least a dozen other advisors who advised me not to miss capitalizing on a crisis. He was planning to reacquire Conductor and he told me I should do the same with Meetup. I shouldn't *go with the flow*, I needed to *create the flow*. I told him that I wasn't like him. I wasn't the founder of Meetup and I certainly didn't have the connections or the personal capital to make the acquisition. He said he wanted to introduce me to Jason, the founder of a major tech company. Jason frequently partnered with CEOs and founders, and he had seen me speak at a WeWork conference and already wanted to back me in the acquisition. I was stunned. Could it be this easy? Well, why not talk to Jason and see how it goes? So, I asked for an introduction.

Jason did his homework and was beyond prepared for our conversation. He knew how to move fast. The first time we spoke, Jason had already decided how much equity he wanted to give me, written up a CEO employment contract for me, and decided how much Meetup should be acquired for. I was impressed. He told me that we needed to act very quickly or it would be too late—ideally, within three days. We should draft a letter of intent to purchase Meetup and send it to WeWork. His attorneys would draft everything, but because he was behind the acquisition of Conductor, he didn't want to be named the front-facing acquirer. I should be the primary buyer instead. While I wasn't particularly comfortable putting a bid in as the buyer backed by an investment group, I came to understand that there wasn't anything illegal or unethical about it and that it was consistent with what WeWork's president encouraged me to do.

Jason wanted to acquire Meetup for $1 million due to the company's heavy financial losses. Why was this even conceivable, you might ask? This had a chance of being accepted only because we had budgeted Meetup to lose around $25 million in 2019. For $1 million, Jason would stem the losses of WeWork and get the business for close to nothing. It's not an unheard-of scenario—there have been companies where the buyer is actually *paid* to take the business off the seller's hands.

I didn't think that was a particularly good outcome for WeWork, but hell, if Jason could succeed due to WeWork's need for speed, I was more than happy for me and Meetup employees to be a direct beneficiary. So, about ten minutes before the start of Rosh Hashanah, the Jewish New Year, I emailed a letter over to WeWork's president and head of M&A that Jason's lawyers had written for me. The letter asked for exclusivity and expressed an interest in acquiring the company within two weeks for $1 million. It was a two-day holiday, and as an observant Jew, I wouldn't be using my phone or any other devices for two days. I would send it out and have no idea of the response.

As the holiday ended, I was eagerly anticipating their response. Perhaps WeWork would say yes. Or they would ask for $5 to $10 million. As the sun set and I was then able to use my phone, I went through my four hundred–plus emails and saw . . . no response at all.

There wasn't even an acknowledgment of receipt. *Well, that's peculiar*, I thought. Maybe my email didn't go through. But it did. I decided to wait another couple of days and then finally got up the courage to ask WeWork's head of M&A what he thought of my offer. His response was that it didn't even justify a response. Ouch! I let Jason know that we weren't in the ballpark. I tried to get him to agree to up the price to $20 million so we could close the deal. He wasn't interested. He was open to going up to $10 million, but I didn't want to insult the WeWork team any further. Jason wanted a deal that presented almost no risk and ended up with no deal at all.

I had grown close to another CEO of a WeWork-owned business, Adam Enbar of the Flatiron School, an online coding boot camp that WeWork had acquired several months before acquiring Meetup. Unlike many founders whose companies were acquired by WeWork, Adam was truly appreciative for all WeWork had done to invest in growing Flatiron after the sale. He was rarely bothered by WeWork's craziness and seemed to always be appreciative of how lucky he and Flatiron were for being part of WeWork. WeWork had invested heavily in Flatiron's growth, and the company was growing at a faster rate than WeWork, despite heavy financial losses.

Flatiron was told that they would be the only acquired business that WeWork would retain. I was jealous. I believed that Meetup was a better business than Flatiron. Why did WeWork want to keep Flatiron and get rid of Meetup? I couldn't help but think that I had failed.

Adam Enbar also recommended that I think like a founder and that I try to acquire Meetup in a management buyout (MBO). To his credit, he introduced me to five venture capital firms with whom he

had a relationship. Even though I didn't have many personal relationships with venture capital and private equity firms, I did have
hundreds of relationships with founders and tech executives. They
could make the introductions, as Adam Enbar happily offered to
make for me.

I now had a decision to make. Would I start to proactively reach
out to venture capital and private equity firms while also meeting
with WeWork-directed acquirers of Meetup, or just be reactive and
complacent? **Be bold.** "Think like a founder, not a CEO!" Founders
go big; I'm going big!

Challenge 27: Is the best way to sell a company to take an iterative approach to contacting buyers or to do a full-on blitz?

Decision 27: Full-on blitz

Time is the enemy. **Be speedy.** Success will be a consistent percentage of my sales pitches, so better to make one hundred or one thousand pitches to potential Meetup buyers as quickly as I can.

I decided I was going to find the acquirer of Meetup myself. Like
my email blitz after business school, I went all in and reached out to
more than a hundred founders and C-level executives and asked every
single one for an introduction to a potential acquirer. I wasn't going
to do a halfway job, and I knew time was of the essence. I wanted to
talk to every potential financial partner as fast as possible, so we could
still use speed to our advantage. I spent the next three weeks working sixteen-hour days, speaking to more than one hundred potential
buyers for thirty to sixty minutes each. While doing so, I also had to
ask myself: Is this sale for me or for our employees?

Challenge 28: What's my real motivation?

Decision 28: It needs to be both for yourself and the business.

There is nothing wrong with creating meaningful value for yourself. Your job isn't to be a martyr. Do what's right for you, but make sure you also **do what's right for the business**. Ask yourself, does it pass the "headline test"? The headline test has always helped me to answer questions of right or wrong. If you would be comfortable having the absolute truth in a headline for all to read, then do it. If not, don't. I've heard others refer to this as the "Exhibit A test." Never put anything in writing that you wouldn't want to see presented as an exhibit in your trial. Since the truth nearly always comes out, if more people use this test, they would get into a lot less trouble. I was comfortable with creating financial value for myself in parallel with value for potential investors and our employees. I was going to find a buyer for Meetup and drive meaningful value for all parties. But to do so, I needed to know the lowest price that WeWork would be willing to accept to divest Meetup. WeWork's priority was a quick divestment and they were more than willing to sacrifice price for speed.

In a negotiation, you must know what will represent a win for the seller. If I could learn what WeWork would consider to be a "win" for them, I was confident I would find a buyer that would see the price as a winning purchase price. I knew $1 million was too low and also knew that WeWork expected to get only a fraction of the $156 million they had paid. So, what's the best way to get WeWork's minimum price? Ask them!

I called Rohit Dave, the head of WeWork M&A and told him that I'd be willing to reach out to my contacts only if I would be able to succeed, and I could succeed only if I knew the amount WeWork would take. The logic was sound, and he told me that WeWork would connect with the board. WeWork's board had an answer: $30 million. Jackpot! That didn't seem very hard. WeWork didn't damage the company to such an extent that I couldn't find a buyer for $30 million when the company had just recently been sold for $156 million. We had about 15 percent more revenue since the sale (though also with huge losses), but I was confident. I could find a buyer for $30 million.

Never enter a negotiation unless you know exactly what you need to achieve to succeed. Having conversations without a very specific goal is incredibly inefficient and makes it nearly impossible to succeed. Know the goal and then work maniacally to achieve that goal. Too often, people just work maniacally to achieve goals that they don't even know they are pursuing.

I asked a few friends what percentage I should ask for as CEO and broker of the deal. Jason had offered me 20 percent of the company, but that was when the sale price was $1 million. I didn't believe that 20 percent was appropriate. It seemed too high.

I called Kevin Ryan, the former CEO of DoubleClick, a twenty-year advisor of mine and someone who has worked with hundreds of startup founders. He told me that 10 percent for myself and 10 percent for our employees sounded reasonable since I was also serving as the banker on the deal and the deal wouldn't happen without me. I told him I felt a bit uncomfortable with such a high percentage relative to all employees, but he was confident that it was an appropriate amount and that I was doing good by employees to get them a 10 percent equity pool. He also said that I should stay in touch and feel free to get his counsel through this process.

Little did I know at the time that seeking his counsel now would result in finding the person who would become the savior of Meetup and the ultimate acquirer. But before I could rejoice in learning exactly what I needed to find from an acquirer, I was confronting the worst public relations disaster of my professional career, causing a Meetup organizer revolt in the middle of a heated sales process. The disaster threatened to both massively decrease Meetup's valuation and quite possibly get me fired in the process. As I had learned and relearned throughout my career, **be surprised only by being surprised**.

Challenge 29: Should you bury a disaster or confront it? Which is better to preserve a company's value?

Decision 29: Confront it.

Apologize fast and take full responsibility for everything. Do not make any excuses. No one cares.

I've always believed that every blessing is in small ways a curse and what may be a curse could be a blessing in disguise. It's important not to immediately react, and evaluate whether a recently painful event wasn't actually the help you needed. The result of a public relations disaster ended up being a major blessing. In fact, it resulted in such a blessing that other buyers accused me of "manufacturing the problem in order to get potentially skittish buyers to drop out of the process," which most certainly wasn't true.

Here is what happened: As I've mentioned, we built a strategy to change Meetup's business model to eliminate the subscription fee to our organizers and charge Meetup attendees $2 to attend an event. Our organizers did all the work; why should they pay as well? Members of Meetups would pay a nominal fee and we would be able to attract many more organizers. Organizers would create more groups and host more events, which would result in more members. It was the exact strategy I had laid out months prior in our company's strategic plan. We had been working on it for six months and were ready to launch. Meetup sale process or not, we believed in it.

Sounds great on paper. But life is not on paper.

We rolled out a tiny test that represented less than one-tenth of 1 percent of our organizers: fifty organizers out of two hundred thousand.

By rolling out to a handful of organizers in Delaware, we believed there was minimal risk and we would then learn from the experience. Unfortunately, we forgot about a little thing called social media. An organizer in the test became so incensed that we would start charging his members and mistakenly believed that we were forcing him to do so (we weren't). He decided to share on every social media platform that Meetup was changing its entire business model. His inaccurate tweet went viral. Within hours, we had tens of thousands of organizers wondering what we were doing and thousands threatening to cancel. Everyone assumed the worst, that we were rolling out a new model, when we were just conducting a small pricing test. Due to WeWork's notoriety (and the press's insatiable appetite to write anything negative about WeWork), nearly every major business publication picked up the story (which was based on inaccurate info) overnight.

Forbes, *Business Insider*, *Fortune*, and about one hundred other publications published the inaccurate information of our plans to start charging people to attend Meetup events. Meetup's dozens of potential acquirers were wondering why we were trying to make a major business model change in the middle of a company sale. We were getting WeWork-like press, and it was hell. As the CEO, I obviously couldn't ignore it. Do you react or respond? Do you double down on your plan or kowtow to some random person on social media and pull back? Do you let them win?

Be pragmatic. You let them win.

The trick to making this decision (and most decisions, really) is to take the "you" out of it. However you feel is irrelevant. Your pride is not what's on the line. Your ego as a leader is not part of the stakes. The only thing that matters is keeping your company's customers.

I quickly issued a public apology, which each publication posted. In it, I affirmed the value Meetup placed in its organizers and customers and said we were not, in fact, making a massive payment change for our existing customers. We were conducting a very limited test, as we often did, and we were sorry that our language caused alarm and confusion. We would continue to consult with our organizers and members, and if we made payment changes, we'd give them plenty of options to meet their various needs and goals, as well as plenty of advance notice of any changes.

We also decided to launch a public campaign called #MeetupLove to combat the negative press we were getting. We asked our millions of organizers and members to share their inspirational stories on social media of how Meetup had personally impacted their lives. And it worked. People shared thousands of positive stories on social media, an outpouring of appreciation that replaced and far exceeded the negative press and remotivated our employees on the power of our mission. We took a terribly negative situation and tried to squeeze the lemonade out of it.

And that was that. After issuing the letter and launching our #MeetupLove campaign, the furor died down rapidly. We ended up with a grand total of only seven cancellations (out of two hundred thousand organizers) that were directly attributable to this situation. For many months, one of the first questions acquirers asked us continued to be, "What the hell was that member pay test you did that garnered so much press?" We continued to need to explain it during the due diligence process, and it probably lowered Meetup's valuation.

We learned two important lessons. First, if you make changes to your ecosystem, you need to be incredibly communicative with partners during the process. It is for this reason that we immediately decided to organize a public blog that would let our organizers have insight into our product- and business-testing priorities. Our blog, now called *Community Matters*, has been read by hundreds of thousands of our members and organizers. Had we not made this mistake, we never would have launched our blog. Second, even if we conduct a tiny test, we need to be incredibly careful about any actions in the public sphere since anything can be shared with millions of members.

For me, all this confirmed my belief that when you're fair and transparent, things will work out.

To sum up, in the next two quarters, you'll see the consequences of your earlier decisions, and unexpected obstacles will be thrown your way. It's often a tough but far more exhilarating period than your first few months at the company. Here are the key takeaways:

- If employees leave, embrace it. This is an opportunity to start fresh with new hires, while retaining the employees who truly want to stay.
- Be honest and communicate with employees about bad news, however ugly it is. Otherwise, employees will hear it from someone else. They will be grateful for the truth.
- If an unforeseen challenge arises, first step back to see the big picture. When WeWork decided to sell Meetup, I had to step back to figure out my role in the sales process. In challenging times, you will have to step back too.
- Seize opportunities that arise in a crisis. Don't let hard times scare you from taking advantage of these unique opportunities.
- Take ownership of the sale process. Sell your company quickly. Talk to as many buyers as possible as fast as possible.
- Be comfortable creating value for yourself. Just don't sacrifice the company's well-being for your own.
- Confront disaster. Take responsibility for it, even if it's not your fault. You will be blamed anyway, so own it.

7

LEADING IN NEW TERRITORY

Now that I knew the guardrails of what WeWork needed and what I was asking for, I could start contacting everyone I knew who was connected to a potential investor. It wasn't about the investors that I knew (which weren't many), but it was about the investors that my network knew. I had always cultivated a large network and aimed to help as many people as I could by using my network to find jobs or hire executives. I've probably made hundreds if not thousands of introductions through the years. Call it karma or call it asking for help, but I was going to **expand my options**.

Challenge 30: How to find an investor

CEOs are expected to be captains of the ship. We're supposed to know everyone's names and how everything works. We pick the star to steer by, and we must get everyone comfortable with following our orders. In theory.

In practice, I was not at the helm of a fifth-rate British frigate. I was an executive at a tech company. So how could I get past one of the key specs for a CEO, finding an investor, when I had never done so in my past?

Decision 30: Work the network.

I would blitz my network and use that as a learning tour.

Most CEOs will tell you that their job is a lonely one. And they are right. Not only do strong CEOs not win any popularity contests, they are usually people who are comfortable being unpopular. Early in my career, I was a less effective leader. I cared too much about what my team and direct reports thought of me. When the annual performance feedback results came out, I wanted to be perceived as beloved. It was great for my ego, but it was not great for company results. The loneliness of most CEOs and thus their need to be liked by their teams is why organizations like Young Presidents' Organization (YPO), Vistage, Chief, and other leadership networks are so important: They provide community. CEOs need a forum to commiserate, share best practices, and understand how typical their challenges really are.

When I was CEO of Investopedia, we were owned by IAC, a company that had also owned Match, Tinder, HomeAdvisor, Angie's List, The Daily Beast, Dotdash, CollegeHumor, and another dozen digital properties. Once a year, IAC chairman Barry Diller would gather all his portfolio CEOs and COOs for a three-day strategy session. Barry Diller is a business and media titan. Being chairman of both IAC and Expedia and founder of Fox Broadcasting Company and USA Broadcasting earned Barry a net worth of more than $4 billion and the sagacious perspective of someone who has seen and learned from thousands of businesses. Barry introduced me to Governor Andrew Cuomo at a private gathering, David Blaine at an IAC offsite, and Michael Eisner and Chelsea Clinton at IAC board meetings. The thoughtfulness of his questions and curiosity in our business was evidence of someone who deeply evolved his leadership style from hyper-aggressive in his youth to hyper-supportive today. At the end of my interview with Adam Neumann, he asked me what his good friend (yes, every NYC tech billionaire does seem to know each other) Barry Diller would say about me. I told him to ask Barry himself. And I got the job. I'm not sure whether they even spoke, but if so, then thanks, BD!

At Barry Diller's annual IAC executive offsite, we would present on our businesses for thirty minutes and had the rest of the time to build relationships with other leaders. As I look back, these annual events were far from wasteful. It afforded each leader the opportunity to learn from some of the smartest business minds in the industry and to build relationships that could last decades. The beauty of the event was that instead of pretending that the goal was about business growth, it was clear that the goal was about letting off steam and building strong relationships with CEO colleagues.

As I mentioned earlier, when I accepted the role at Meetup, one of the selling points for me was that because WeWork had acquired three or four other businesses and would be acquiring many more, there would be an opportunity for relationships with CEOs of WeWork portfolio businesses in the same way that I had at IAC. Through these and other experiences, I had built a strong network of digital leaders and knew that I could ask my network for assistance in finding potential acquirers.

There would be no "bad" conversations. I was **long-term focused**. Every conversation would be a referral to a different potential buyer. Yet time was of the essence. I had two weeks to find a buyer who could commit $30 million to buy Meetup. In parallel, about sixty potential Meetup buyers had reached out directly to WeWork. So, I reached out to everyone I knew who was connected to a private equity or venture capital firm. I spoke to partners at Sequoia, Greylock, Bessemer, Rho, Matrix, Insight, TPG, Stripes, General Atlantic, Warburg Pincus, Blackstone, Riverside, Cove Hill, and dozens of others. I signed fifty NDAs in about a week, emphasized a sense of urgency to each and the high investor return of a $30 million Meetup acquisition, and went from having no idea what I was doing to still having no idea what I was doing but at least having fun doing it.

The feeling that I could control my destiny was intoxicating. I was waking up at 5 a.m. ready to work for sixteen hours a day. I had my normal CEO day-to-day job, WeWork due diligence meetings, and my own Meetup acquirer quest. I've never minded working long hours for short periods of time. I've always prioritized work-life balance, but I could handle an insane schedule for two, three, or four weeks—and often that schedule is a hell of a lot of fun, as long as it is temporary.

I learned a tremendous amount about smart decision-making during this short time. Some lessons:

1. *New perspectives from really smart people are invaluable.* Having spoken with dozens of venture capital leaders, each of whom had evaluated hundreds of companies, I could tap into the collective brainpower and experience of thousands of companies. And the more conversations I had, the more that the same themes emerged and the same advice was dispensed. I had the great fortune of having a "board of directors" of hundreds of industry leaders, and if nearly every advisor was saying the same thing, well, they were right and I was wrong. Nearly every advisor told me that despite the previous small layoff that we still had way too many employees, and that one of our business areas also needed to be shut down since, although promising, it wouldn't be profitable for years. This served as the basis for my decision shortly after these conversations to let go of about 30 percent of our staff and shut down one of our businesses. And both were the right decisions.

2. *Find an investor whom you actually like.* I met with more than a hundred potential partners, and many were, simply put, not people with whom I would want to partner. While some were interested in continuing conversations, I decided that life was too short to spend time with an investment partner with whom I didn't connect. **Be**

long-term focused. Despite a strong personal financial incentive, I gravitated toward those with whom I had a strong personal chemistry. I decided to trust my gut, and if my gut told me it wasn't going to be the right fit, I was taking enough probiotics that my gut health was strong enough, and I should listen. Call it the "probiotics" test.

3. *Investors are often driven to invest in a company more because they believe in the CEO than because of their confidence in the business.* Fred Wilson is perhaps the most influential NYC-based venture capitalist. He and I had the opportunity to meet a few times during the sale process. Because he had been on the board of Meetup previously, he was very familiar with the business opportunities and shortcomings and was interested in acting very quickly. He and I hit it off, and he told me that the main item keeping him from acquiring Meetup was detailed due diligence on what he considered the most important consideration at Meetup: me. I was taken aback that he deemed me so critical, but he said that ultimately when he invests in a business, he is investing in the CEO. The CEO ultimately makes the decisions about the executive team, company strategy, and priorities. It all came down to confidence in and the capability of the CEO.

I anxiously awaited the outcome and then started hearing from not one or two but five, then six, then eight different individuals whom he spoke to about me. In all, he took the time to speak with close to a dozen people. And his response to me: "David, you're a polarizing figure. Some people—in fact most people—love you. But some of the people I spoke to really don't like you. I need to pass." I explained that I have fired more than fifty execs through the years and made decisions that weren't always understood—but my explanations were to no avail. He was out.

There are some great lessons here. If Fred Wilson, a true venture capital icon, is willing to speak to a dozen individuals about me, I should spend a lot more time researching our company hires via back channels. His time is certainly a hell of a lot more valuable than mine. Also, always do your best to preserve your reputation even when you need to let leaders go. Those damaged relationships will come back again, as they did for me, and can hinder your future success. These are tough lessons but important ones.

4. *The right incentives can dramatically impact a deal.* Jeremy Levine, a partner at Bessemer, is one of the most well-respected tech venture capital investors. I had a few connections to companies he had invested in and was able to get a thirty-minute meeting with him. Right from the start, he told me he wasn't interested in Meetup. I knew I wasn't going to persuade him, so I quickly pivoted and asked for his advice. He told me that I should be asking WeWork for a deal fee. I hadn't thought of that before, as I was already getting paid to run the company, and my responsibility as the CEO was to sell the company. He explained that it was just as much in WeWork's benefit, if not more, for them to incentivize me to maximize the sale price, and that their investment in giving me—and potentially other members of our management team—a percentage bonus for the sale would have a direct ROI for WeWork. He told me that I was actually doing a disservice to WeWork in not asking for it.

I left the meeting pumped. He told me to ask for 10 percent of the sale price. He, too, emphasized what I had learned earlier, that there is nothing wrong with creating meaningful value for yourself and it doesn't need to conflict with what is best for the company. In fact, it can be argued that a highly motivated and incentivized CEO can also drive more value for all company employees.

Ten percent would be an enormous sum of money. Although I am **bold**, I didn't have the guts to ask for that much, but as I was walking back from his office and before I even got back to our office, I called

WeWork's head of M&A and said, "I should be getting a deal fee and it is in WeWork's interests to do so. Incentivize me and our team to be 100 percent focused on maximizing the sale price for WeWork, and everyone wins." I used Jeremy's exact advice. WeWork's head of M&A then told me I should propose something to him. I proposed a far less lucrative suggestion than Jeremy had suggested to me—and was flatly rejected. I was told that it would set too much of a precedent for the other businesses that WeWork was trying to sell to give me and our management team a percentage-based incentive, and he could provide only a flat-rate, small fee upon close. I quickly accepted, as it was better than nothing. I also asked that another executive get a bonus for her efforts, and that was approved as well. I was glad I had asked in the first place—you never get what you don't ask for—but WeWork's decision was without a doubt the wrong one. WeWork would have likely netted tens of millions of dollars more had they been generous in providing a sales incentive to our management team. It wasn't the first or the last time WeWork would exercise poor business judgment.

Their decision to provide a few of our leaders a flat-rate fee upon the sale made us completely indifferent about the sale price. In fact, it put my personal incentive at odds with WeWork's ability to maximize its sales price. The higher the price a buyer paid, the higher my and all employees' strike prices would be on our future options, which means the lower the potential payout would be for all of us when the buyer looked to sell Meetup again in a few years. More importantly, the higher the price a buyer paid, the greater the growth expectations and pressure on me and our management team to achieve outsized growth as fast as possible to justify the high price. This intense pressure often decreases the likelihood of long-term success. See WeWork as Exhibit A on how intense growth pressure can destroy company value.

The management team and I now had both financial as well as psychological reasons for why a lower price was preferred. WeWork had the exact opposite incentive and obviously wanted the highest potential sales price in divesting Meetup. However, from an integrity standpoint, I was paid to sell Meetup to the highest bidder. I made the decision that integrity and fiduciary responsibility must be prioritized over personal gain, and I proceeded to meet with more than twenty firms with whom WeWork had our team interact so that my team and I could persuade potential buyers to acquire us. It was an incredibly painful and conflicting situation and one that could easily have been avoided with the right incentive system for our team.

5. *It's OK to stand up for yourself, your company, and your employees.* While I didn't feel comfortable prioritizing personal financial gain over WeWork directives, I was comfortable prioritizing what was **right for our business** and best for our employees. A strategic buyer and pseudo-competitor met with our CFO and me. During the conversation, he informed us that his first action would be to lay off the entire management team, including myself and the vast majority of employees. His plan was to fold Meetup into their company. It would likely be the end of Meetup as an independent brand. Another financial buyer told us that their goal would be to get Meetup down from the current two hundred employees to fifty as quickly as possible and asked whether I was "up for it." These were lines I wasn't comfortable passing. I simply couldn't aggressively try to sell the company to a buyer that would mean my personal demise and the termination of our entire management team, most of our employees, and our business.

One of my colleagues, another CEO of a WeWork-backed business, took an alternative approach. He refused to meet with a single buyer whom WeWork had initiated. If WeWork wanted to sell the company, then they would do so without him. I was impressed with his all-or-nothing approach. I considered it, but I just didn't have the guts to go to that extreme a position. I later learned that another CEO did the same. I was actually in the minority of CEOs of WeWork-acquired companies who were willing to meet with potential buyers.

I informed WeWork that they were free to continue to pursue some of the buyers, but that I was not comfortable being in the meetings and trying to sell the company to buyers who would effectively end Meetup. WeWork wasn't happy. They told me I needed to take the meetings. They informed me that a CEO was going to be flying in from the West Coast and I would need to meet her. I refused again. I let WeWork know they could fire me if they would like. But I knew they wouldn't. If you are trying to sell a company, the last thing you want is a company with no CEO and massive upheaval in the management team following a CEO termination. I had the cards and played them, and they shut down both conversations that would have led to Meetup's likely demise.

I decided to make it clear to WeWork which companies I preferred as acquirers and which I was opposed to. I even received a call from Sebastian Gunningham, WeWork's new co-CEO, asking me to rank each of the potential buyers in the order of what was in Meetup's best interests. WeWork understood that the more aligned I and our management team were, the greater the likelihood a deal would close, and if a deal closed with management support and continuity, the lower the likelihood of potential chaos and litigation post-sale. But WeWork still refused to build the right incentives—and that would lead to terrible consequences once COVID-19 hit a few months later.

6. *Turn a crisis into an opportunity for your employees too.* I had a unique opportunity to meet with more than a hundred venture capital and private equity leaders to learn about how to turn the company around, and there was one piece of advice I was getting over and over again. We still had too many employees for the revenue of our company.

Fortunately, Michael Kellman, a close friend and executive at Stride Consulting, was looking to hire as many strong engineers as he could, and he told me that his company would be willing to interview 100 percent of the employees we laid off for any role at their company or with their clients' companies. As our employee population cares so deeply for each other, I knew this act would provide meaningful support for those terminated as well as an important signal to our remaining employees that we are a community that looks after each other. Even during the sale of the company, I still made sure to **work for the employees**.

I saw that just as we could address the crisis by going big or going home as a company, we could do the same for those who would be leaving it.

So we gave our employees a spreadsheet that included the names and contact information for hundreds of hiring managers and companies. And WeWork was incredibly generous in severance packages—so generous that numerous employees asked to be included in the termination. We didn't want some of these employees to leave but we also didn't want to hold them hostage. The combination of each of these tactics led to very fast, empathetic actions that rightsized our company, made it a more attractive candidate for an acquisition, and led to significant support by our employee population.

I received an email from one of those employees that brought it home for me:

Date: November 15, 2019 at 12:00 PM EST

Hi David,

I wanted to let you know that I really appreciate what you're doing to help me with this transition. I've been taking advantage of the fact that I can for once in my life devote 100% of my time to finding my next option. I've already spoken with a dozen companies and recruiters and have several second round interviews on the calendar. Right now I'm pretty optimistic that I'll be able to turn lemons into lemonade.

I hope things are settling down a bit at Meetup although I know there's more to come with the move and the sale. I'm still rooting for you to turn Meetup around even if I'm not there to help you get there and I hope our paths cross again in the future.

Best Regards,
XXXX

An important message in decision-making: If you need to do something difficult, always do it as humanely as possible. I've said it before, and I'll say it again: **Be kind**.

7. Fewer employees can enable faster iteration. After terminating seventy-five employees, about 30 percent of our company, my initial thought was, *How in the world can we get everything done that we need to do?* To my surprise, we moved faster. This may shock many, but we genuinely moved much faster with fewer people. The reasons are important to understand, as they can help any leader determine whether scale is speeding the company up or slowing it down:

   • Fewer toxic employees: Meetup had a number of key employees who were incredibly focused on the company's mission but with little interest in revenue or business success. The company also had a lot of negative-focused individuals who would say things like "We tried that three years ago and it didn't work," or "Here are all the problems with your decision." We kept people who were less experienced but had a positive outlook. We kept people who had a strong bias toward solutions even if those solutions weren't the right ones.

- Focus: We eliminated product teams that required significant coordination that actually slowed us down. We shut down our entire staff in Berlin because communication proved inefficient. We deprioritized product features that wouldn't move the needle.

- Hiring: When a company is hiring a significant number of engineers, then senior engineers are spending a disproportionate amount of their time on interviewing and onboarding and not on building a great product. When there is no hiring, leaders can focus on getting work done.

- Eliminating the layers, red tape, and functions that existed only to facilitate communications: Certain roles get work done while others slow work down. We disproportionately eliminated more roles that were about minimizing risk than those focused on growth.

Leaders are always looking to accelerate their team's ability to achieve and surpass goals. Sometimes it is in having fewer employees, not more, that this can be achieved.

8. *Find a way to step off the treadmill when it's running too fast.* So much had happened in the weeks since I was first informed of the Meetup sale that I didn't have time to think or take a step back on what I was doing and even why I was doing it. As someone who is naturally competitive, I knew that I wanted to "win," but I didn't even know what I wanted to win or why. And how much of my focus was for personal gain and how much was in the best interests of Meetup? What is the more important personal gain—is it financial or the opportunity to have greater autonomy and/or impact?

Should I take actions that are actively worse for me personally but potentially better for Meetup?

Despite the tumult surrounding me, I decided I needed to take a half day and just be by myself. A short break, even in busy periods, is justified for those who are **long-term focused**. There is a lake with a hiking path near my home in Westchester County, New York. Alone in nature is my ideal environment for taking stock of my priorities. During my walk I decided that my top priority was finding an investor group whom I trusted. Trust was more important than direct financial gain. Jack Welch, thank you. I also decided that even though I didn't know the outcome, I would find a way to exert significant influence. I also decided that I would **expand my options** and be open to conversations outside of my role at Meetup. I knew that if I had other options to consider, I would psychologically be more comfortable not proceeding with Meetup if another interesting opportunity were presented. I would be more objective and therefore make a better decision. Finally, I decided that if my leading Meetup wasn't in the best interest of the company, I would **do what's right for the business**, by offering to find a new CEO for the buyer and stay on for a temporary, transitional period.

While I couldn't find the time for even a full day off (or more likely I could have, I just didn't prioritize doing it), taking just a half day to question my motivations and goals proved to be extraordinarily valuable.

9. *Asking for advice is the best way to get a meeting.* I set up more than fifty meetings with top global venture capital partners, but not to pitch. Pitching in an email is a recipe to get a no. Instead, I asked for advice. It's also why asking for informational interviews can make a real difference for younger job seekers and open doors for their futures.

Because most of the meetings were introductions made by my network, I believed that the best way to ensure potential acquirers were willing to meet with me was to appeal to their ego—as well as their genuine interest in helping me. By asking for advice and their further recommendation on who to talk to, it built a deeper relationship and led to further conversations. My typical opening line was something like, "WeWork bought Meetup for $156 million a couple of years ago. We now have 15 percent more revenue and I was told from WeWork's board that they would approve a $30 million offer to close quickly. What advice would you give me on how to secure an investment group as quickly as possible?" Inevitably, they would recommend themselves.

10. *Understand the strategy and goal of your investor.* The approach of meeting with anyone and everyone did have a significant drawback. Every firm I spoke with was intrigued, and we would have a few conversations only to find out later that Meetup's size, growth profile, or lack of profit didn't fit their firm's investment strategy. It was still the right approach, as I got great advice about our company and built relationships that would last me for years. Had I been more experienced, I would have asked about the fund's strategy far sooner in the conversation, but asking for advice made for helpful conversations. Ask for advice, and you build a relationship instead of a onetime conversation about an opportunity. I learned, but I did so at the expense of efficiency. If I learned more about a company's investment goals, I would have saved a lot of time. Bottom line: Do your research.

11. *Every challenge is an opportunity for you to be better at your job.* Having to conduct more than thirty due diligence meetings also presented an enormous benefit in helping me nail down our company's strategy and my narrative around it—both of which

are critical for a CEO. I had relatively recently joined, and because the company was in such chaos when I started, I spent most of my time on HR- and strategy-related priorities and didn't have sufficiently deep knowledge of the detailed metrics and key performance indicators that drove our business. Being forced to go through hundreds of hours of inquisitional due diligence sessions for buyers drove a profoundly deeper understanding of our business fundamentals. Our due diligence meetings with buyers became like an orchestra by the time our management team was doing its twenty-ninth and thirtieth meetings. It felt great to understand our business drivers as deeply as we did—and has led to much smarter decisions in the many months since. I've always been a fan of *forcing mechanisms*. And my forcing mechanism to better learn the financial, operational, and product details of our business was these meetings.

12. *Regardless of how busy you are, family is always a higher priority.* In the middle of all the tumult and due diligence meetings, I was faced with a dilemma. I had booked a long weekend with my fifteen-year-old son to head to a Green Bay Packers game in Wisconsin and would miss a day and a half of work. And two weeks later, we planned a short family trip to visit my eighteen-year-old son in Israel. Most people assumed I was going to cancel both trips, as we were in the thick of negotiations. The thought of canceling, however, never entered my mind. A sale may take many months to resolve. Putting my life and family on temporary hiatus should never be an option. Taking this time away (though I still was forced to work while traveling) was not only important but also reenergized me to be able to persevere through the months to come. Leaders need to take time for themselves. Our jobs are incredibly stressful, and doing so ultimately saves time and makes everyone more productive.

13. *The most important question: "Whom else can I speak with?"* We don't ask for help enough. When looking for a new job, we are afraid to impose on our friends and former colleagues. When looking for a new client or a partner, we are uncomfortable asking for referrals. My advice: Get over it and get over it quickly. People genuinely want to help you. You are doing yourself and the helper a favor by asking for help. And the best way to ask for help is to ask for others with whom to speak. At the end of every conversation I had with the dozens of potential Meetup buyers, I asked, "Whom else can I speak with?" Everyone wanted to help; I sent thank-you notes and the results of their referrals afterward. Always ask for help and know that the best question you can ask is whom else you can talk to.

Challenge 31: Facing failure

The result of working sixteen-hour days for three weeks and having hundreds of hours of conversations with venture capital and private equity partners was . . . nothing! I couldn't get a single firm to agree to acquire Meetup.

I failed again. Now what?

Decision 31: Failure is a great lesson. Move on.

Who cares about failing?

Virginia senator Mark Warner has always been an inspiration for me in the value of failure. He was the first person in his family to go to college. He went to Harvard Law and then didn't have any job offers. His first business failed in six months, his second in six weeks. He was reduced to couch surfing and living out of his car. And then he got on the ground floor of a little company called Nextel and became a self-made millionaire. As Senator Warner said, "My success was due to good luck, hard work, and support and advice from friends and mentors. But most importantly, it depended on me to keep trying after I had failed."

I had twenty interested firms, then ten, then five, then three, then one, and then none. I couldn't believe it. I had "the deal of a lifetime"—one-fifth the price that WeWork paid for Meetup—and I couldn't find a single investor. The most common reason for being rejected had nothing to do with anything I could have controlled or directly impacted. Firm after firm repeated the same message to me: "We like you. We love Meetup, and the ROI on the deal could be compelling. But Meetup doesn't fit our fund's investment profile." In order to persuade investors in a venture capital or private equity fund, the leaders of a fund typically create a very clear investment thesis and are then forced to adhere to that thesis. Some potential investors told me that they couldn't invest in Meetup because Meetup was too big; others said it was too small. Some told me that Meetup wasn't profitable enough to fit a fund's investment thesis, and others told me that it also didn't need enough capital. Some funds invested in only specific industries and others in early stage only. I had spent countless hours trying to convince buyers who were intrigued enough to take a meeting with me but were ultimately unable to be convinced to invest. I was crestfallen.

Bids were due in two days and not only was I not able to use speed to my advantage to prevent others from bidding, I wasn't even able to find an investor willing to bid more than my initial $1 million bid from a month ago. So sad.

I consoled myself in having made a gallant effort and that my three-week blitz with hundreds of potential acquirers was far too short a time to find a buyer. In the end, however much I had learned, I failed.

I had reached the point that no leader likes to reach, when they're faced with the question, now what?

You can't despair. You can't let previous failures sidetrack you. You must keep trying. Sherlock Holmes was guided by the idea that once you've eliminated the impossible, whatever remains, however improbable, must be the solution. So if you believe there must be a solution that can be found, and you should, then look to the improbables that you previously disregarded as impossible.

Case in point: There were a few firms who had contacted WeWork, and WeWork had decided that they weren't serious. I asked the head of WeWork's M&A team if I could essentially take their scraps and speak with anyone they rejected. I was given two names. I spoke to each, and one individual, Chad (not his actual name), wanted to partner with me to submit a bid. I didn't know him. He had no LinkedIn profile—a major red flag—and I had no time to vet him. What kind of a business leader doesn't have a LinkedIn profile? I should have ended the conversation right there, but I had to **be pragmatic**. I was desperate to stay in the game. I asked him to give me the names of three references, which went directly against my back-channel-only rule, but I couldn't even try researching him myself since he was publicly invisible in all social media. I spoke to all three names he gave me. One was a personal friend of his, another was a business partner, and a third was someone who worked for him in the past. They painted a picture of him that was relatively positive but hardly overwhelmingly so. If someone could choose any three people to provide a reference, I would expect the references to be outstanding. His were not. More red flags.

I then told him that I couldn't partner with him unless we first met in person. To my amazement, he said he would get on a flight to New York the next day and we would have an opportunity to spend time together in person before submitting a bid. I was definitely impressed by his tenacity. In our one-on-one meeting, I decided to take a very specific approach to see how he reacted. Instead of building a rapport by talking about common interests, I wanted to see whether he was driven by ego or could be an effective partner and listener. I had assembled a list of five positive themes and twenty areas of concern and opportunities for improvement from the three conversations I had had with his references. I didn't hold back. I went item by item and asked him about each of the twenty areas of concern. And he finally blew my mind. He wasn't defensive at all. He acknowledged his past mistakes with total humility. He said that he thought he would learn more from me than vice versa and that he would fully support and take my lead in making decisions. He was earnest, and it was clear to me that he wasn't always this way but had failed enough times that he truly knew his strengths and development needs.

I remembered that my priority was finding a buyer from whom I could learn and with whom I had strong chemistry, but I decided that it was more important to submit a bid with someone whom I didn't know at all just to "stay in the game." Now wasn't the time for ideals; it was about surviving as a viable bidder. If I submitted no bid, I was out. As long as I submitted a reasonable bid, then WeWork would continue to engage me as a buyer. I was able to get Chad, after one conversation, to submit a $30 million bid. I had absolutely no idea if he had $30 million or if he could raise $30 million, but it was a Hail Mary and I decided to go for it. Whatever happened, I would **be surprised only by being surprised**.

It was now early December 2019. WeWork was in complete disarray. Adam Neumann was out, and the new co-CEOs had purged the company of any executives who had close ties to Adam. My manager Dan Teran, who was close with Adam, was part of that purge. WeWork announced plans for massive layoffs, and no one knew whom to go to for anything. I now had no manager, I had secured a partner I didn't know to submit a bid, and Meetup was still losing significant cash every day. I even started hearing rumors that WeWork was considering just shutting Meetup down as they had done with another one of their acquisitions. The one straw of optimism I had was that I could submit a bid, in the final hours, for the exact amount—$30 million—that I needed to win.

WeWork had dragged me to dozens of meetings with potential buyers, the vast majority of whom I knew full well had either no real interest or no capability in acquiring Meetup. An example of this was a breakfast I was asked to attend with Jonah Peretti, the founder and CEO of BuzzFeed. It was well known, due to rounds of layoffs in the company, that they had little financial flexibility to acquire Meetup. Nevertheless, WeWork was insistent that I join a breakfast with their CEO. We proceeded to have a pleasant breakfast that was devoid of any meaningful conversation about the acquisition. The next day, an article came out that BuzzFeed was looking to acquire Meetup. Every company had its motivations for talking to us and apparently BuzzFeed's was to try to make itself relevant and in the news. This was one of the many distractions that was unhelpful at a time of significant employee stress.

Fortunately, WeWork told me we just needed to submit a $30 million bid to be given exclusivity. We submitted the bid and I was eager to get this behind us.

And then another surprise.

I was misinformed, by a lot. Our bid wasn't even close. Perhaps our management team and I had done too good a job in our due diligence meetings with the many WeWork-initiated buyers, and to my and WeWork's utter shock and amazement, there were seven bids above my $30 million including five that were more than double my bid and one that was close to triple.

Well, at least I tried—and in some ways actually had succeeded. I was able to submit a bid for my $30 million target. I also realized that there was now little chance I would be staying on as the CEO of Meetup. Any acquirer would be bringing in their people and a new management team. I had enough experience to know how that went.

After serving in operational roles for the last twenty-plus years, I now had a Rolodex of one hundred venture partners and private equity partners I met through this process, and I could reach out to them and see if they were looking for a venture partner in their firm. I quickly then backtracked and decided that jumping to another company before seeing this through made no sense. The relationships were there, I could reach out in a month or in six months, and I wanted to see how this would play out and how my short but eventful time with Meetup would ultimately end.

I then made an impetuous mistake. I got an email from LinkedIn asking if I were open to receiving interest from other companies who wanted to hire a CEO; the email stated it was confidential and only hiring recruiters would hear about it. I carelessly checked the box and agreed. Within twenty-four hours, I learned that a previous employee who was in recruiting saw that I was "open to new opportunities." *She took a screenshot* and forwarded it to all her previous colleagues at Meetup. An employee whom I trusted let me know that nearly every employee in the company saw a screenshot that I was "open to new opportunities," and the general sentiment was, *Well, if he doesn't believe in Meetup and isn't going to stay, then why should I stay?* They didn't realize that the employee who had the highest likelihood to get fired now was me—and nearly every Meetup employee had more job security than I. I quickly revised my LinkedIn status and it further solidified an important lesson: The CEO is always under a microscope. Anything you say, do, or don't say or do will be interpreted and often misinterpreted. Know that you are always being watched. If you aren't comfortable with that, don't be a CEO.

On the flip side, the same is true for potential owners, and while I thought my tenure wasn't likely going to be long term, I could still ensure that Meetup got the best future owner. This would guide my thinking through the next big challenge I would face: vetting our potential buyers.

Challenge 32: Should you readjust your goals once you know all is lost?

WeWork's preferred buyer, the top bidder, would be terrible for our management team and Meetup's future.

Decision 32: Patience over speed

This is when patience is needed over speed. The truth nearly always comes out. Just give it time, and an unstable individual or unscrupulous company will implode on their own.

WeWork proceeded to move into exclusivity with the top bidder. It was a private equity firm based on the East Coast and led by an investor who had been organizing Meetup events for more than a dozen years. The potential buyer had a banker, significant financial backing, and a track record of closing deals very quickly. All parties were confident a deal would close before Christmas, and I was getting ready to figure out how much time I would take off between jobs and what I would do as an unemployed executive during the holidays.

After signing the exclusivity agreement, WeWork set up a full day of due diligence with the buyers. It was both a disaster as well as an incredible blessing.

The disaster: The buyer group represented a deal leader who was a minority financial investor, backed by a midsize private equity firm. The deal leader, Leni (not his real name), was somehow, in the span of a six-hour meeting, able to anger nearly every Meetup executive with whom he interacted. He could not simply **be kind**. Instead, his arrogance was on full display throughout the day. Typically, buyers are on their best behavior during a due diligence meeting. They are trying to build relationships with the executive team in order to build support among them prior to a deal happening. Buyers know that although the final decision-maker is WeWork, it is in a buyer's interest to have the CEO and executive team excited and on board with the new owners.

Toward the latter half of our meeting, I informed the senior M&A person from WeWork that we were no longer going to proceed with due diligence if he continued to insult and berate our team. We would walk out. From that point on, Leni sat quietly, didn't say anything, and likely spent the rest of the meeting planning how he would replace each of us.

Initially, again, I felt helpless. WeWork was going to sell Meetup to whoever was going to pay the most for the company. That was a completely reasonable decision. If they sold the company to a jerk, while bad for Meetup and our management team, WeWork would cash the check and wash their hands of us.

But was I actually helpless? Should I go along with this deal for the sake of WeWork or find another approach for the sake of Meetup? And if the latter, how?

I decided I wasn't going to just let this happen. I would **be bold**. I forced the buyer into a decision of their own.

I called the partner of the private equity firm (Leni's financial partner) after a couple of days and said that if Leni was going to be involved in the company, I would be leaving. If I left, then our management team would also be leaving. If the management team left, then there would be chaos and all of 2020 would be spent managing the chaos. Again, I framed the entire rationale in what would be beneficial for the firm. I knew the firm didn't care about me or Meetup. In trying to persuade senior leaders, unless you have a deep relationship with them and can appeal to a higher calling, don't bother. **Be pragmatic.** Always return to the core basis for how leaders make decisions: their personal interests.

I also called WeWork's new co-CEO Artie Minson, with whom I did have a close personal relationship and mutual respect. I told him about Leni's behavior. I explained that chaos would ensue if this buyer were successful and that when a company begins to fall apart there is greater chance of litigation. I framed each of the conversations in the best interests of each party—WeWork's interest as the seller and the private equity firm's interest as the buyer. There was no reason to frame it in my own or Meetup's interest. I knew that was secondary—or not even secondary—to getting a deal done at a high price and quickly.

The partner of the private equity firm understood that I had set up a binary decision—either proceed with Leni or proceed with our management team; there was no other option. So, the partner chose a third option—and decided to back out of the deal. Yes! Disaster again averted—now only six offers ahead of our $30 million offer. I didn't realistically think we had a chance with our offer, but I was trying to land Meetup in the right future owner's hands and knew that Leni was not it.

The blessing and lesson: While dealing with Leni's behavior was incredibly stressful, in many ways it presented a significant blessing to our team. We learned his true intentions and behaviors. What would have been far worse was for him to act like a decent human being during the selling process only to turn into a maniacal egomaniac after the sale. This is a critical lesson: Witnessing bad behavior and seeing how candidates, partners, and potential managers act during times of stress is crucial to deciding whether to join a company or forge a business partnership. There is a saying in the Talmud that a woman shouldn't marry a man until she sees how he acts in his financials, when he is angry, and when he is drunk. It is only in seeing people at their most challenged moments that we should make significant business decisions. We created an intense environment where decisions had to be made quickly. Leni's behavior shone through fast and we avoided a terrible "corporate marriage."

Amazingly, I then learned a few days later that Leni was not done. He still had exclusivity and found a new financial partner in a New York–based private equity firm. WeWork told me that while Leni lost his first financial partner, he still had another week left in his exclusivity. I was incredulous. WeWork was still perfectly happy to work with Leni since he was the path to maximizing the sale price. I informed WeWork that if Leni had any direct conversation with me or anyone else in our management team, then we would refuse to participate in the due diligence. WeWork understood, as did the New York City–based private equity partner. I, however, believed that while Leni would be absent from any conversations, he would be lurking in the background and ready to assume the chairman—or perhaps my CEO—role as soon as the deal was inked. Now I had to get this next partner out as a buyer. It was Leni 2.0.

WeWork organized a breakfast for me to get to know the new partner. It was a great first meeting. During the meeting, I **was honest**. I shared some of the stories of Leni's behavior. He then said that because Leni had brought him the deal, he wasn't able to proceed without him, but if WeWork told him that they didn't want to proceed as long as Leni was involved, then he could follow up with Leni and find a path to removing him from the picture. WeWork complied and it worked. Leni was officially out—and this time it was final. WeWork then proceeded to move into the second exclusivity with a new private equity firm, and we organized another full-day due diligence session with the management team.

Unfortunately, I now discovered that I'd pulled Meetup out of the frying pan only to land in the fire. Again. Private equity was looking more like a private nightmare.

Challenge 33: If you are an influencer, how can you have more power than those with actual decision-making authority?

I was neither the buyer nor the seller; I had no power; yet I had more influence than anyone.

Decision 33: Turn the tables.

When interviewing for a job, turn the tables and interview your manager. When selling your company, interview the buyer. I needed to find a way to turn the due diligence process upside down and go from influencer to decision-maker myself.

During the next all-day due diligence meeting with WeWork's now top choice, we were able to understand the strategy of the buyer. It was put simply: Gut the business. Fire as many people as possible. Maximize profit and sell it quickly. We also understood their area of greatest concern—our technical debt. As I mentioned before, *technical debt* is a term used to explain a company's years of short-term technical decision-making that compound and drive so much technical complexity that making a simple change on a website or app can take weeks or even months instead of days. Significant technical debt developed at Meetup as a result of our product teams taking thousands of shortcuts over our eighteen-year history. Our technology became an unusable Swiss cheese of dozens of programming languages and millions of lines of code. It was a deep disenabler to our success.

After the due diligence meeting, I decided that this next private equity firm was also not the right Meetup owner, as they would be solely focused on cost reduction and short-term profit maximization. I didn't believe that the right path was to threaten I wouldn't stay. I had already done that once, and WeWork wouldn't tolerate my doing this again. I needed to understand their cause of greatest concern—and be incredibly honest about it. I believed that as long as I was completely honest and transparent, then highlighting potential buyer concerns was not an ethical breach. This presented an interesting ethical question.

Typically when trying to sell a company, you focus on highlighting every possible way a seller can spin a challenge into an opportunity. "Imagine how much faster we can grow once we improve our technology." Or, "Once we focus on improving our technical infrastructure, we'll see massive user growth."

Is it unethical, however, to be brutally honest? We did have a serious tech debt issue; was it inappropriate to be incredibly transparent about it? Or does it simply make me less effective at sales, and as long as everything that is shared is 100 percent true it passes the integrity "headline" test? I thought about Cuisine AuntDai, a Montreal restaurant that gained notoriety for its brutal honesty. "We are not 100% satisfied with the flavor now and it will get better really soon," is how the menu describes their mouthwatering chicken dish. Then adds: "PS: I'm surprised that some customers still order this plate." It was this honesty that has driven the restaurant's success. I decided there was nothing wrong with brutal honesty that may have negative short-term implications.

I suggested to our VP of engineering that he be as transparent as possible in sharing both the opportunities and challenges in our extremely problematic technical debt. If the new buyers still wanted to acquire the company, at least they knew what they would be getting. We had our technical diligence call and he was extremely honest about the company's many challenges, opportunities, and the time and cost it would take to remove our tech-debt challenges.

Within twenty-four hours, the new buyers bailed.

WeWork wasn't happy about the situation. It had now been six weeks and two parties had dropped out of exclusivity. By having to go back to the other bidders, WeWork knew the other bidders would smell weakness and lower their price. And they were right.

I was at this point thrilled. We had jettisoned Leni, we had avoided the next buyer who wanted to shrink Meetup down to nothing, and while there were still another four bids ahead of ours, there was a remote chance that other bidders would drop out until we found a great partner that would truly invest in Meetup's future growth and success.

The lesson of how influential one can be with no direct power continued to amaze me. I was neither the buyer nor the seller. I wasn't the founder or an investor, but somehow as the leader of the company, my ability to have a significant impact on the outcome was deeply empowering. I actually began to feel like Meetup would find its perfect owner. I was wrong, again. But, as always, I was **surprised only by being surprised**.

Challenge 34: What do you do when your goals are divergent from your owner's goals?

How can you reconcile the two?

Decision 34: Don't even try.

There are myriad reasons for divergent goals. Understand the reason for each but once you and your board have different goals, it is time for one of you to leave. And likely it will be the CEO that is packing their bags.

The next top two highest bidders for Meetup were a Chinese private equity firm who wanted to replicate Meetup's business model in China and a private equity firm in Texas who during due diligence asked me why we had fired only 75 people when we should have let go of 175 people. Oy.

Another two firms wouldn't be focused on growth but would instead focus on driving down costs. This sounded eerily familiar. At times I started to believe that if every firm felt we should just reduce Meetup to its bare necessity team, perhaps they were right and I was wrong. Upon closer examination, they were right—for their goal, which was to minimize risk and maximize likelihood of a short-term return on their investment. The question of reduce cost versus invest is an incorrect way to evaluate "right versus wrong." It was all about goals. Based on the private equity firms' goals, they were right. Based on my goal of maximizing Meetup's impact on the world, I was right and more investment was required. We had strong differences of opinion because we had divergent goals, not because one of us was right and the other was wrong.

I wanted to dedicate my professional life to driving Meetup's ability to change people's lives and make the world a better place. Meetup uses technology to get people off of technology and drive real, human connections between those who would never have had an opportunity to meet before. So much that pains the world is based on a lack of access to learning opportunities—and Meetup democratized that access so that anyone, most often at no cost, can learn nearly anything. So many deep and institutional problems in the world are based on ignorance and people's lack of exposure to those who are different from them, leading to widespread—and growing—racism, xenophobia, and hatred. And the deep relationships that Meetup facilitates break down the ignorance that all too often pervades people who do not know one another.

So much of what ails society is related to loneliness. Although the global loneliness pandemic has gotten worse since the onset of the COVID-19 pandemic, loneliness was a huge societal problem well before that. Thirty-six percent of people in the US who were polled prior to the pandemic regularly felt lonely, and among current and recent college graduates (Gen Z) the global rate of loneliness is as high as 62 percent. Meetup is the cure for the loneliness epidemic and the world's technology, social media, and gaming obsession. David Brooks spoke directly to Meetup's impact in a keynote at Brandeis University's 2011 commencement: "Over the past few years, we've learned a lot about happiness. We've learned that the relationship between money and happiness is weak. Once you hit the middle class, getting richer isn't going to make you that much happier. The relationship between friendship and happiness is strong. Joining a club that meets just once a month produces the same happiness gain as doubling your income." Meetup was that club for millions of people, and getting millions more to be impacted by Meetup was my goal.

I didn't have the same goals as these private equity firms. I wanted to be a part of changing the world and I was happy to take on greater risk and have less confidence in a big payday if it meant there would be a far greater likelihood that we could invest and grow Meetup so it has ten times the global impact it has today.

I have found that whenever there is a deep disagreement in tactics, it is nearly always because there are disagreements about the goals. I wasn't aligned with these firms' tactics because I had a different goal. As managers and leaders, we need to diffuse tensions around divergent tactics by asking our teams to align on the exact goals that we are trying to achieve in the short and long term. Most often, the tension will then dissipate, and a team can move forward.

Challenge 35: What do you do when you have no good options?

Should I accede to our new buyer's goals, impose my own, or find some middle ground? Should I instead somehow find an alternative to these two potential offers and obviate their goals entirely?

Decision 35: Make a new option.

I couldn't refuse to meet with the next two highest bidders—though I considered doing just that. It was now late December and we had two ninety-minute calls with each where we provided an update on the business. As in the past, I decided to be incredibly honest and transparent so both WeWork and potential buyers knew the current situation. When WeWork (the seller) needs to go back to potential buyers, it is a signal that the seller is now weaker. That often enables a buyer to seize the opportunity to lower their bid. Unsurprisingly, each of the two parties lowered their bids from about $75 million to $60 million. Well, $60 million was now only double mine and Chad's

$30 million bid. Perhaps we had a chance if both bidders also decided to pull out of the process.

I didn't think I had the strength or psychological wherewithal to go through another two exclusivity periods and detailed due diligence meetings. Besides these two, there were another two bidders above my and Chad's $30 million bid. I decided to contact Chad for the first time after not speaking for two months (due to confidentiality clauses in our exclusivity agreement, we were prohibited from speaking to each other until this point).

Chad was surprised to hear from me, as he assumed that all was lost. I told him that we had one last shot. If he could get his investors to $60 million, then I'd **be confident** that WeWork would give us exclusivity and we could jump ahead of the four other parties who were ahead of us. At this point, WeWork genuinely wanted to sell Meetup to the buyer whom the management team wanted. They knew that we would work far harder to close the deal and maximize the certainty of close if we were aligned on our choice of the final buyer. Again, it was important to present what was in Meetup's best interests as fully aligned with WeWork's interests.

I needed to find a way to convince Chad to raise his offer to $60 million from our $30 million initial bid. Chad called his investors. That type of increase meant both double the up-front cash but also half of the potential return that investors were expecting. I knew it was a long shot, but as with before, you never know unless you try.

He called me back and said that it was impossible for him to get his investors to go from $30 million to $60 million in only a few days. But we both wanted the opportunity and he said he'd commit to WeWork that we would pay the $60 million in a revised letter to WeWork even though he hadn't yet raised the capital. He hadn't in fact even raised the $30 million in capital, so committing to $60 million wasn't much of an issue since all of it was capital he didn't actually have yet! Fortunately, while WeWork knew that Chad may not have all the capital needed, they wanted to believe he did, as did I. WeWork is notoriously an optimistic organization and their naivete was a benefit of this optimism. Chad and I believed that if we were granted exclusivity and worked hard, we'd be able to find other investors who would come into the deal to get to the $60 million. We just needed the time to do so, and with exclusivity we would have that time. This was, again, our only shot. While we had gone in and out of two exclusivities, it didn't seem likely that we would be able to remove the next two parties from contention as quickly. Chad agreed with my assessment, and despite not having the funding, he sent a revised letter of commitment to WeWork for $60 million.

That Sunday evening, in late December, I received a call from Artie Minson, WeWork's co-CEO. He said, "David, if Chad can get his deal to $70 million, it is his. You and your team have been through hell and back and we want you to get what you want." I knew that WeWork wasn't excited about either of the other two options. One was a Chinese firm whom they believed would face significant regulatory requirements and for this reason would take a long time to close. The other was a firm who was notorious for lowering its price after entering exclusivity. Despite our goal of winning the bid, it was important not to now chase an offer and be desperate. I called Chad and said, "Don't give in. We can win this at $60 million. You don't need to go to $70 million." Chad agreed. We held firm. WeWork relented—as we had expected—and accepted our bid. We now had a twenty-calendar-day exclusivity period. It was ours to lose. There is an important lesson here. Know when the other party in a negotiation is asking for more simply because it can't hurt to try, rather than because there is a true competitive threat. Chad and I knew that there was no credible threat, and we held firm and won exclusivity.

It was now January 2020, and things were finally looking brighter. The shine would, however, darken very quickly as, unbeknownst to all of us, the global pandemic had already started its march forward. **Be surprised only by being surprised.**

But before we go on, let's recap. After the first year in your leadership journey, you'll inevitably encounter many, many unforeseen problems. Here's how to wade through these uncharted waters:

- Rely on your network. You may not know what to do, but your network does.
- Move on after failure. Learn from it. And try again.
- Be patient with people who cause you trouble. These troublemakers often implode on their own.
- Turn the tables. You can still influence the final outcome of a decision, even if you're not the one with the power to decide it.
- Align your goals with those of your owner. If you cannot, one of you must leave.
- If you're offered no good option, make your own call. You don't have to accept what you are given.

8

FACING THE UNKNOWN UNKNOWNS

Any leader can look at a situation and devise a plan. All leaders conceive of likely scenarios and prepare responses based on previous experience in similar scenarios. What do you do, however, when all your plans are laid to waste by something impossible to foresee, an unknown unknown, and you have no idea what the future will bring? Pushing your company through that problem is the real test of a leader, as I discovered when dealing not with the sale of Meetup, but with COVID sweeping across the world, first in China, then to Italy, then to every one of the 193 countries where Meetup operates.

Surely the coronavirus wouldn't come to the United States, we thought, and if it did, there was no way it would have much of a real impact on our business. SARS didn't. The West Nile virus didn't. Not even Ebola did. None of these prior "pandemics" had any impact whatsoever on Meetup. Boy, were we wrong.

We started seeing our Meetup events (all Meetup events were in person) shrink in COVID-impacted countries by 20 percent, then 30 percent, then 50 percent, and then 90 percent—all within a week. The negotiations for Meetup quickly changed too. Overnight we lost nearly all of our committed investors.

WeWork was even more scared of COVID's impact on the company's cash flow and became increasingly more desperate to offload Meetup. By this time, WeWork was also in all-out chaos mode and fearful of how COVID would directly impact their own core business. The last thing they wanted to think about was Meetup. WeWork told Chad that they were now willing to accept a $25 million offer, less than half of what they demanded and believed they could have received from four or five other bidders. In just a few weeks, as January turned to February, Meetup's perceived value had fallen by more than half.

Chad now had only two investors who weren't terrified about COVID and could provide the capital to acquire Meetup—and one of them was Bill Ackman. Ackman is one of the world's most notorious activist investors with thousands of articles painting him as a shark that eats other sharks. I was told that he was eager to help Meetup for philanthropic reasons but also because he believed that Meetup had no direct competitors and, if run well, could one day be a unicorn—have a billion-dollar-plus valuation. I was nervous, nonetheless. I told Chad that I could already see the headlines: MEETUP: FROM THE HANDS OF ADAM NEUMANN TO THE CLUTCHES OF BILL ACKMAN. I told Chad that working with Bill was a terrible idea. His reputation preceded him. Chad asked me to keep an open mind and still meet with Bill.

Bill, Chad, and I met, and despite my preconceived notions, I found Bill to be honest, affable, and an excellent listener. I was shocked. I decided to call a few leaders whom I believed may know Bill better than I. I went back to my mentor Kevin Ryan again. Kevin was the founder of *Business Insider*, Gilt, MongoDB, Zola, and a dozen other companies. Surely he would know the real Bill Ackman. And Kevin did know him, not well, but enough. Kevin said, "Actually, he is a good, decent guy."

I learned a valuable lesson. The press loves to create heroes and villains, and just like in pro wrestling, one can become the other if it serves the narrative. Adam Neumann was the hero of WeWork until he wasn't, having done nothing different. Bill Gates was bad, then good, and now back again to bad (especially if you are a QAnon believer or think XP was good enough). Elon Musk, bad. Steve Jobs, good. You get it. Meet the person, then decide for yourself.

Challenge 36: What do you do when presented with all bad options?

A sequel: Endanger Meetup but preserve myself by selling to Bill Ackman or find yet another investor?

When your back is against the wall, should you just choose the least-worst decision?

Decision 36: Hang on and hope a better one appears.

I came to realize that my fortunes and Meetup's would be intrinsically linked. What would be good for Meetup would be good for me, and what would be bad for Meetup would be bad for me. If you don't trust someone to invest in your company, then don't trust the person to be on your board either.

I had now heard great feedback about Bill and enjoyed spending time together. I was a go. The only open item was to be sure that Bill was aligned with the compensation package that Chad and I had agreed upon. I believed that, like me, Bill was **long-term focused**. I also believed that he had nearly unlimited access to capital and would look to me for leadership around running a tech company. Unlike many investors, Bill fully understood that tech was not his forte. Then things got a bit strange.

Thus I was confronted with a sequel to a previous challenge: Having figured out how to get the most out of the sale for me and my employees, should I endanger the sale to Ackman to preserve my own compensation?

That Saturday night, Bill texted me that the deal was done and he had negotiated directly with Sandeep Mathrani, whom SoftBank had installed as the new CEO of WeWork after the co-CEO arrangement following Adam didn't work out. I had no idea he was even speaking to Sandeep—I had never even spoken to him myself. No one in the company knew him. I wasn't sure that Sandeep even knew that WeWork still owned Meetup, having many more issues to deal with at WeWork than divesting Meetup. My relationships had served me well throughout this process, but I had no idea how to have a conversation with Sandeep, who now completely controlled my and Meetup's fate.

Bill Ackman, however, had found a way. Sandeep agreed to sell Meetup through an apparent digital handshake and a few texts. Apparently, though I can't confirm whether or not this was the case, Bill was responsible for helping Sandeep get his big job as CEO of Sprint. After six months, would the final decision on Meetup come down to Sandeep having a prior relationship with Bill? I called Chad and learned that Bill, ever the negotiator, decided that $25 million was now overpaying and he wouldn't pay more than $20 million for Meetup. He told Chad that he wasn't going to serve as the lead investor at Chad's $25 million price. If Bill was out, Chad no longer had the funds. Bill knew that and told Chad that he would invest only if he could negotiate directly with WeWork's new CEO. The result of that negotiation was a verbal agreement between Sandeep and Bill to sell Meetup, and that Chad would be removed as the primary point person with WeWork. Chaos ensued. WeWork's M&A team, which had been working on the Meetup sale for six months, was completely left out of the conversation and no one knew who was talking to whom. WeWork's M&A team was still talking to Chad. Sandeep was talking to Bill. No one was talking to each other, and I certainly had no idea whom to talk with. All I knew was that Chad was now out as an intermediary and Bill texted me that the deal was done.

If Chad was removed as an intermediary, I was fairly certain that I would be removed as the CEO, or at least my employment agreement I had negotiated with Chad would be nullified. It seemed too late to try to wrestle Bill away from acquiring Meetup, so my only option was to accept our fate and confirm my new employment agreement with Bill and get the deal closed. I decided that I didn't want my agreement to be changed from the one I had with Chad. Bill was now getting a far better deal and he could afford my meager salary relative to his potential outsized payday. The next day, Bill and I had a Zoom chat. It was the last week of February, the market was heading toward its fourth straight day of losses, the Dow had already plunged more than a thousand points due to COVID fears, and he had already fled the city and hunkered down in his Hamptons home like thousands of his financial colleagues.

As we were talking, I saw his head turn toward the right every thirty to sixty seconds. After close to a dozen of these head turns, I asked, "What do you keep looking at? It's kinda distracting." He said, "1.5, 1.6, 1.7." I had no idea what he was talking about. Apparently, right before our conversation, he had placed one of the largest hedges in the one-hundred-year history of the market and the value of his hedge was increasing from $1.5 billion to $1.6 billion to $1.7 billion. Normally I would find this amusing, but because we were going through my compensation package, I found it deeply disturbing that he was at the same time pushing back on nearly every single item. It seemed to me that he was arguing for the sake of arguing and negotiating as a tactic rather than toward a specific goal. I didn't like it. I've always believed that "dating is a great prerequisite for marriage," and the way an individual behaves prior to a deal will only be worse after the deal. Will he be examining every decision that I make? I informed him that Chad and I had already agreed on my compensation package and I wasn't interested in changing it. He then asked me to email him the lowest compensation package that I was willing to accept.

On March 7, I sent him back the exact same employment contract I had agreed to with Chad as my minimum. No changes. **Be confident.** If I was going to get eaten by the shark, it would be as a shark, not a minnow. Apparently, Bill didn't appreciate that move and informed his co-investors that he would be looking for a new CEO. I knew there was no chance they would find someone strong in the next couple of weeks, so I encouraged them to start looking for someone else but said that if they wanted to have me lead the company, then as a matter of integrity I needed to keep the same deal that I had agreed upon initially. As a leader, you need to know whether you are holding the cards in the poker game of life, and if you have the winning hand, then be sure to go all in on it. So, I went all in. The key to being willing to go all in is being completely comfortable with the outcome. Bill had asked for substantial changes to my agreed-upon offer and had also asked for substantial changes from Chad in his deal terms. I didn't believe I'd enjoy working with Bill, as a pattern had emerged, backed by his past reputation. I was fully comfortable walking away if needed. For that reason, I was comfortable playing a strong hand.

And they folded.

Bill became increasingly distracted with the historic market turbulence as the coronavirus was creating pandemonium and he began to walk away from the deal. I had been told not to worry about Bill and that he would quickly get distracted and not micromanage Meetup. But I was surprised he was so easily distracted right in the middle of the negotiations of a handshake deal he had already made with WeWork's CEO. Chad had lost Bill as an investor and had lost every one of his previous investors but one, who was willing to put only a couple of million into the acquisition. In a month Chad went from theoretically having $60 million in commitments to $2 million.

Chad went back to WeWork again and it became clear that the price had now fallen to the unthinkably low price of $10 million, with WeWork wanting to retain 10 percent. I later learned that this 10 percent retained ownership is commonly referred to as schmuck insurance. This is the idea that no company that divests a business wants to look like a fool should the business then rebound and be worth five, ten, twenty times the value. At the very least, the business can retain 10 percent and participate in any upside should that happen.

The problem, however, was that Chad wasn't able to assemble $10 million as the coronavirus was wreaking havoc on Meetup—the largest *in-person* community and events platform in the world. By mid-March, our events volume, new subscriptions, event RSVPs, and nearly every metric were down 60 to 80 percent. While our revenue, due to our subscription business model, was stable, it was inevitable that would fall quickly too.

We had gone too far and come too close to just lose everything. **Be surprised only by being surprised.**

It was now the second week of March 2020, and in an irony of ironies, Meetup was one of the first companies to be ejected from its WeWork offices. The second case of COVID in New York City was found in one of our employees, and as of March 10 we were all homebound. The press feasted on this. We were about to get sold, had no corporate office, were losing tons of our members and organizers, and faced the possibility of WeWork deciding to shut us down immediately. WeWork's finance team had already calculated the costs of doing so, and it seemed only a matter of time until I got the phone call they would do it. Maybe we should go back to that $1 million offer from many months ago?

In a last-ditch effort, I decided to reach back out to Kevin Ryan, the same person whose counsel I had sought in the early days of the deal and whom I had also asked for advice on Bill's reputation. At one point, he had told me that if the price became a "no-brainer opportunity," he'd be interested and able to move quickly. Kevin only invested in startups and had never acquired a business that was like Meetup, with its eighteen-year history. It was against the entire strategy of his firm, but he was also a savvy business leader and understood that if there is an opportunity, one should not stand on ceremony and ignore it.

Chad then told me he had a second investor and could come up with a total of $6 million. I called Kevin and told him we had a very short time frame and the deal was now in "no-brainer" territory. The company had sold for $156 million and was now 15 percent larger and much more profitable and 90 percent of Meetup could be acquired for $10 million. Chad's extended exclusivity was about to end and I asked Kevin if he was interested in coming in for $4 million. I quickly sent over any historic information we had on the company, most of which was largely irrelevant due to the massive impact COVID was having on the business. Nearly all in-person events were being canceled globally and our organizers were canceling their subscriptions at a record pace. We were offering discounted subscriptions and free short-term subscriptions (COVID would be done in a month, right?). Despite the rapid downward trajectory of our business, Kevin told me within twenty-four hours that he was in. He signed an agreement to join our investment group.

Kevin is very well respected in the tech industry. He has been a leader, if not *the* leader, of the New York tech scene for more than two decades. For this reason, Chad and I asked Kevin to call WeWork directly and tell them that we were now able to move forward and get the deal closed within the next week. WeWork trusted Kevin.

Except we weren't actually ready to close. Chad actually had only $4 million. We needed to pay WeWork $10 million and we needed to put at least $2 million aside for future expenses. We needed $12 million. Kevin and I were incensed, as we had already agreed to all the terms in the offer based on Chad providing more than half the funding and Kevin providing the rest. Kevin then agreed to put in about $8 million in exchange for a number of additional concessions from Chad. We were aligned and now just needed the final confirmation from WeWork and would close the deal in a few days. Kevin told me that this would be one of the largest investments he had ever made in any company and the least due diligence he had ever done on any company he was to acquire. He said he believed in Meetup's mission and he believed in me, and that was enough for him. Trust really did go a long way and it was this trust that Kevin had in me that confirmed that I would be able to trust him fully as well.

Challenge 37: How to persevere under extreme exhaustion

It ain't over till it's over. WeWork had one final surprise bidder up its sleeve.

Decision 37: Keep your eye on the prize.

Exhaustion doesn't matter when you know the end is near. You can always rally when the end is days away. What is true of work is often true in life. It has even been proven that prior to a sick individual passing away, they, too, rally and are often most alert in the days and hours before their end. Hopefully, however, this was not Meetup's end.

WeWork surprised us again. WeWork had been keeping another party in their back pocket all along, but I had no idea that they had been negotiating with them so extensively or that the party was so viable. WeWork smartly wanted to re-create a competitive situation to try to regain some of the significant potential value Meetup had recently lost and to pressure each side to close faster. It had been a part of every due diligence meeting and I was sure I knew the other party. It was a small, private acquisition entity run by Willie Hutton (not his actual name). Willie's bid from six months prior was one of the many bids above our initial bid. He and I had built a strong relationship during the due diligence process, and he told me that a valuable strategy for acquiring assets is to simply "hang around" and stay close to the sale, irrespective of whether the sale took months or even years. He was now the only competition left to get the deal.

I called Willie and he gave me two substantial increases over my personal deal with Kevin and Chad. Willie was now giving offers to me instead of WeWork, which was an interesting twist. He first offered to double the equity position that I had agreed upon with Kevin. He also told me he would make that equity guaranteed as long as I didn't quit within four years. Even if I were fired, I would have enough upside to be able to retire while I was still in my forties. While blown away by the offer and despite having a positive perception of Willie both as a person and business leader, I rejected his offer with no hesitation. This wasn't the time to be clouded by personal self-interest.

On top of that, I had decided that my priority was working with an investment partner whom I trusted without a shadow of a doubt. I had known Kevin for twenty-two years, and he was willing to acquire the company with virtually no due diligence. I liked Willie, and he seemed trustworthy, but I didn't really know him.

I asked Willie why he would offer such an outlandish proposal and Willie said something that truly floored me. He said that he spoke to WeWork's head of mergers and acquisitions, and WeWork had decided that whomever I supported would get the deal. I was neither the buyer nor the seller. I wasn't an investor and had no previous ties to Meetup only eighteen months ago, yet WeWork was adamant that they would let me make the final call. So I did. Despite the greater security and compensation Willie could offer, I chose Kevin and integrity. Easy call.

Competition is a powerful motivator and isn't used enough as a leverage point by leaders. Competition can galvanize a team and drive a sense of urgency that can result in meaningful business growth. When I was an executive at Everyday Health, its founders were true experts at using WebMD as its hated rival and looking for any opportunities to compare our performance to theirs as a galvanizing force in driving marketing or sales performance. Competition provides a benchmark that naturally competitive individuals (most leaders) can seek to surpass.

Leaders must find ways to harness competition to motivate themselves in similar ways to WeWork bringing in Willie to negotiate against Kevin's offer. But competition is a motivator, not the reason to make a decision. Understanding when to use it and when not to is critical. Few smart decisions are made out of fear of competition, but many poor ones are made that way.

Challenge 38: When to trust your gut

I then received another, more urgent call from Willie. He asked to talk directly to Kevin and to join forces so that WeWork would be unable to pit one offer against the other and extract the highest bid. He would come in as another investor in our deal.

Should I nullify WeWork's negotiating strategy by including Willie, or should I listen to my gut, which was saying that would be wrong?

When do you trust your gut instead of logic in making a decision?

Decision 38: Always

Trust the gut. It is easy to get greedy, especially when the money could be life-changing, but the truth always comes out and I wasn't comfortable with this passing my "headline test" of integrity.

I'm no expert in contract law, but it didn't sound kosher to join forces. And even if it was legal, it didn't feel like the right approach. Leaders need to trust their gut when it comes to ethics. Regardless of what may or may not be allowed, if something doesn't feel right, don't do it. It is never worth it. I told him I'd follow up with Kevin but that I didn't feel great about the idea. Kevin and I chatted and Kevin was even more emphatic than I was that he didn't want to have any conversations with Willie prior to the deal. Kevin again demonstrated the type of integrity and professionalism that excited me about partnering with him. I told Willie that I'd be happy to connect him with Kevin after a deal should we get the winning bid but we didn't want to have any potential conflict. Here are a few learnings from my negotiations:

1. *Being unselfish in negotiations can result in the most self-serving results.* I haven't mentioned the one remaining investor of Chad's that didn't abandon us, namely, Joe Steinberg. Joe is a sage, modest, professional investor whom I liked the moment we first spoke. After our issues with Chad, Joe wanted to be sure the deal got done and was willing to sacrifice his equity and short-term capital to support Chad and enable Kevin to agree to new deal terms. Joe went so far as to negotiate a deal for himself that was worse in order to find alignment between Kevin and Chad. After the deal closed, when it came time to determine who would be a part of board meetings and other final decisions, Kevin and I made sure that we did whatever Joe would find most helpful. Joe **was kind**, and his unselfishness built him a lifetime of positive karma that both Kevin and I are eager to repay.

2. *Making sure your partner is capable may be even more important than personal chemistry.* Once Kevin's attorneys reviewed the legal documentation and other closing documents for Meetup's sale, there were massive gaps in what Chad had organized. I didn't have an alternative initially and didn't want to drop my partner in the deal but I also didn't appreciate how Chad was unable to get the deal to the finish line either.

It had now been a long seven months since that fateful call informing me of Meetup's sale. Willie decided to pull out of the deal once he knew he didn't have my support, leaving Kevin and me as the last ones standing. We now had three different law firms—one representing Chad and the original legal contract he created, another representing

Kevin, and the third firm representing WeWork hammering out the final details. Each time WeWork shared that they weren't willing to give on a key item, they ultimately caved. Each law firm was now going to make north of $300,000 on the deal. A good outcome for all involved except WeWork. But WeWork made its own bed. I had no sympathy for them, especially after what they did next.

Challenge 39: How to communicate big news

How do you communicate such a saga to employees?

Decision 39: You don't. Keep it simple.

Keep your communications simple. Be as organized and planful as possible and frame everything on how the sale will directly impact each employee. Follow the WIFM principle in all employee communications. I first learned that at DoubleClick, twenty-two years ago, when I first worked with Kevin Ryan. And have applied it consistently ever since. Share the WIFM with employees, and that is their primary initial focus.

What's WIFM? "What's in it for me."

I received a frantic call from WeWork at 4 p.m. on a Friday, informing me that I needed to call an emergency meeting immediately of all Meetup employees, letting them know that the acquisition was final as of that evening, March 27. You can't make this stuff up. At every turn, no matter what the situation, WeWork's incompetence was somehow able to turn the most banal and straightforward of situations into absolute chaos. With WeWork especially, I was **surprised only by being surprised**.

Meetuppers had been working from home for weeks and having a remote Zoom meeting to announce the sale to employees was about as suboptimal a way to celebrate as you can get. Cobbling one together with no planning at 4 p.m. on a Friday was not how I wanted to start the company's new chapter, introduce Kevin as our chairman, and answer the many questions our employees would have.

WeWork's M&A team told us that due to a glitch in WeWork's human resource management system, if we didn't let employees know about the sale as soon as possible, an automated email would be sent at midnight to all employees letting them know they were no longer WeWork employees. There would be mass hysteria. Again.

Previously, I'd delivered bad news immediately before my fellow Meetuppers could get it from an outside source. I'd also put in place a half-formed strategy instead of a fully formed one to keep things moving. Based on these earlier decisions, should I call a half-assed meeting to announce the sale now or push back and find another way to handle it?

Each challenge is different, so while a previous decision might guide you, you don't have to do the same thing you did before. While I had acted fast in the past, acting fast now would be frantic, not fast, and there is a very big difference between the two. In this case, I refused to hold an all-company meeting that afternoon. I would not rush what had been nearly eighteen painful months as the CEO and seven emotionally draining and tortuous months of a sales process. I needed—and, more important, our employees needed—to hear this exciting news in a way that would motivate them and create a safe environment for changes to come. There must be a way to stop that automated email from going out at the stroke of midnight!

I called WeWork's CEO, their head of HR, their head of legal, head of M&A, chief technology officer, and anyone who could possibly figure out a way to update their HR system. After a few hours, WeWork was able to find a way to fix the notification. Typical WeWork. No regard for employee impact and reaction. Total lack of capability to operate in the most basic of ways. It was a perfect goodbye to a highly imperfect company and relationship. It represented all that I found distasteful about WeWork. The company was filled with incredibly intelligent and thoughtful individuals, but as a culture, those thoughtful people created a system that cratered under the exponentiality of its growth.

The new Meetup was going to be different. We were going to build the processes and systems to support our team's decisions, enable creative approaches, and reward extraordinary performance. We were going to **work for our employees**.

I also learned that if you know something makes no sense, it's OK to **be bold** and push extremely hard—well beyond the point of annoying others—to fix and save people a lot of agitation. **Be kind** always and let the chips fall where they may.

Finally, we were done. We sent an email to all employees late Sunday night, March 29, about a "big announcement" at a meeting the next morning. I found a WeWork T-shirt (not the one I'd traded for, unfortunately) and I slashed out their name with masking tape and started the Zoom meeting by dancing with all employees to "Freedom!" by George Michael. Then I took off the WeWork shirt to reveal my Meetup T-shirt underneath, and all the employees started screaming and clapping.

We were done, we were safe, and we had a future we would create for ourselves. I told our employees that every individual would now be a future owner in Meetup, as a healthy employee option pool was granted by our new chairman, Kevin Ryan. Kevin then spoke to our company, sharing his passion for Meetup's mission; his relationship with our founder, Scott Heiferman; and his commitment to supporting us in the tough months during the pandemic. I shared my favorite story about Kevin: About a decade ago, I had asked him what he was most proud of in his career, and he told me it was that more than one hundred CEOs had come out of the early days of Double-Click since its founding in the late 1990s. Amazingly, Kevin had met

Meetup's founder, Scott Heiferman, twenty-five years ago, and Scott was delighted that Meetup would be in Kevin's safe and trusted hands for years to come. A fairy-tale ending rarely happens, but while we knew we had a long road ahead of us to fulfill our mission of driving human connections and community for billions of people around the world, it didn't look unlikely now that we were finally holding our futures in our own hands.

Before we end this chapter, however, I pause to clarify the key takeaway. Eventually in your time as a leader, you'll be blindsided by a crisis. Mine was COVID. Who knows what yours will be? No matter the crisis, here are the key tips to handle it:

- Hang on. Sometimes, if you just hang on, the problem will resolve itself.
- Remember that the end is near. You can fight exhaustion when you know it's almost over.
- Trust your gut when it comes to ethics. If something doesn't feel right, don't do it.
- Keep the story of how you resolved the crisis simple. People mostly care about how they are directly impacted.

9

RELYING ON YOUR MISSION

I value the power of community because I have lived it. Growing up in an Orthodox Jewish and religious household, community was a way of life. When there was a death, the entire Orthodox community gathered, bringing food to the bereaved family and visiting while the family sat shiva at their home. Community also meant joyous celebrations of marriages and births. These religious traditions date back thousands of years. As an adult, I have also found community through my children's schools, my career, and other avenues of life. Community has played an integral role throughout my life. Meetup is a company focused on building community. Meetup understands that we become better when we're around other people and meeting in person.

Meetup was created by Scott Heiferman and three others immediately after the fall of the Twin Towers, literally in the ashes of 9/11. On that day, when Scott left his apartment, he saw hundreds of people hanging around his apartment lobby having no idea what to do with themselves, but knowing that they didn't want to be by themselves. Scott met residents in his building he had never met previously. He then said to himself, *It shouldn't take a tragedy like 9/11 for people to understand the importance of community.* And that was the founding of Meetup. Meetup would enable anyone to build and find their own community.

The coronavirus, an even greater tragedy than 9/11 and even greater during its heights than a 9/11 every day, may have disrupted Meetup's method of building communities, but it didn't disrupt Meetup's mission any more than WeWork's sale of Meetup did. In fact, it emboldened us. People needed their communities and connection more than ever.

The sale was closed and a new chapter and challenge began. And the trouble was that the obvious way to bring people together—through online-only events—was anathema to Meetup. In fact, through Meetup's history, the primary reason that Meetup would reject an organizer was because they didn't want to build an in-person community. We organized only in-person events—not a great business model during a pandemic!

Meetup has always recognized that the magic that happens when people get together in person can never be replaced online. Scott Heiferman, our founder, even took a sledgehammer to a VR device at a major WeWork conference in order to drive home the message that "We use technology to do one thing only: to get people off technology. That's our goal."

Challenge 40: When do you need to direct a major pivot of your company?

Should we pivot to allow online-only events, despite that going against the very soul of the company?

Decision 40: Pivot when you lose alignment with your mission.

Ultimately, we realized our mission wasn't really about in-person events. Our mission was about keeping people connected.

So we pivoted.

Our goal was now to *use* technology to build community. Of course, this required me to be a more directive leader than I typically prefer. We didn't have time to debate the merits of building digital communities and Zoom events. We had just been sold, our very existence as a business was again at stake, and I knew we hadn't gone through the tumultuous ownership of WeWork, a dizzying sales process, and a pandemic to hold sacrosanct a belief that could lead to Meetup's extinction. I needed to make a decision on my own and I needed to **be pragmatic**. I decided that we needed to embrace online events. This required taking people off their current priorities to enable online events at Meetup as quickly as possible. No engineers or product managers are happy about needing to completely blow up their current priorities, but at the same time, they all understood the criticality of the decision. In fact, the decision was nearly unanimously embraced. We had to be comfortable producing a minimal viable product (MVP) for online events at Meetup that didn't necessarily provide an amazing user experience but was good enough for our millions of members to start with, and then we'd improve it from there.

We were in "wartime" yet again, and if we were honest and acknowledged that we had launched an MVP and why, then our members and organizers would appreciate the rapid pace we pivoted and understand that improvements on the product would be fast followers. Just acknowledging a behavior that is suboptimal is incredibly important. The "people always know," and if you are going to play by a different playbook and choose not to empower teams (which is often the right thing to do), it is best to acknowledge that and not hide from it.

Online events were up and running in less than a week. We spent the next month and a half making many improvements to the experience. Organizers could use any videoconferencing platform to create an online event—and we have had more than one hundred different platforms that have been used. We had running groups who had events where individuals did solo runs during the pandemic and then had their community members get back together for an herbal tea of choice to discuss their runs and meet in real time, albeit remotely. We had board game groups convert to online Yahtzee or online Codenames. We had tech groups go from having thirty attendees in one city to hundreds of attendees across dozens of countries.

While it was pretty hairy going during the first months of the pandemic, this pivot to online events (while still enabling safe, outdoor, in-person events) enabled me to develop six principles of a successful pivot that could guide your own decision-making.

The Six Principles of a Successful Pivot:

1. *Remain grounded.* Just as in basketball, when you're pivoting, you need to keep one foot firmly on the ground. *You can't pivot your mission. You shouldn't pivot your vision. You shouldn't pivot your values.*

   An independent study from ImpactED at the University of Pennsylvania discovered that 89 percent of Meetup's organizers felt that Meetup positively impacted people's lives. An impressive 90 percent of our members felt they gained knowledge and skills when they attended Meetup events. Meetup makes people's lives better. The more Meetup events people attend, the happier they are. That's a beautiful thing.

   So we remained grounded. We said, "Our mission is empowering personal growth through real human connections. Not necessarily in-person, but real human connections is what it's all about. And online events fully fit into that mission."

2. *Support your pivot with best practices.* Make sure to surround your pivot with as many different best practices, communications, and education as you can to really help people understand everything.

We had to educate every single organizer on how to transition from in-person to online events.

How can you run a marathon online? Well, the answer is people can run independently, then get together afterward on Zoom to share a beer. They can still find social connections online. Some events are easier; some are more challenging. We created workshops for organizers, a blog called *Community Matters*, discussion groups, mentoring opportunities, and online event templates to help our organizers pivot to online events. Conversation is the ideal form of communication, so we invited all our organizers and our most engaged members to a new forum we created called Meetup Live. We talked to our organizers about the pivot, what the pivot can create, and why we were pivoting. We have had more than one hundred thousand collective attendees to these educational events.

Challenges are ongoing as many of our members find themselves battling "Zoom fatigue." This is partly technology-related but also the result of not interacting directly with others. The key is to make events as interactive as possible. Make sure every event has an opportunity for breakout rooms, use something like the Icebreaker app to get people to meet beforehand, play games, ask each person their favorite country to visit after the pandemic, and things like that. Make sure there's lots of interactivity between events to get people talking.

We also pushed our organizers to try to get together in person safely during the summer and fall while the weather in much of the world is nicest. There were tons of events, such as book clubs, knitting groups, wine tasting, and thousands of others where masked members could sit six feet away from each other. The key was to figure out how to do outdoor activities that were safe and do online events that were interactive. We also provided disclaimers and instructions about the criticality of following CDC regulations to ensure that all organizers prioritized safety more than ever before.

3. *Understand what is happening in your ecosystem.* When you're making your pivot, you need to understand your users and what's happening in your ecosystem, then pivot more toward that. An example is in early June when we saw an enormous number of Black Lives Matter (BLM) groups created, we leaned into this heavily in terms of a pivot opportunity.

   We decided to make every social justice–focused group free to organize on Meetup. We wanted to make sure we are a platform that supports racial equality, and we now have tens of thousands of members in these groups.

4. *Focus on the future, not just the present.* In your pivot, make sure you're doubling down on future opportunities and not just focusing on your current challenges. To this end, we announced that college and graduate students and anyone with an .edu email can become a free Meetup subscriber for six months. We ended up seeing more than one hundred thousand people attending events with the thousand-plus groups created through our college initiative, Campus Community. It's been really meaningful to our growth.

   If you don't have cash, then you can't make long-term decisions for your company. Fortunately, due to our acquisition and new investors, we had enough cash protection and have only added to our cash during the pandemic. We saw a swing of millions of dollars in our cash position improvement from operations in 2020 versus 2019. We didn't have to focus on short-term revenue. And we didn't have to placate a chaotic parent company. Our priority was ensuring the vibrancy and growth of our ecosystem.

People will attend an event that's free. More than 80 percent of people that become organizers are those who started as frequent Meetup members who, ultimately, a week later, a month later, or a year or two years later, create Meetup groups themselves. It is this longer-term flywheel that would be our core focus after the sale. Our focus would not be chasing short-term revenue or an impossible $1 billion Adam Neumann revenue dream.

5. *Leverage your data*. Meetup has tons of data, including the percentage of in-person versus online events throughout the pandemic. Generally, we can see countries that are handling the pandemic well have a higher percentage of in-person events compared to countries facing serious challenges.

   In the example earlier, our data showed a sudden increase in BLM groups created, prompting us to focus on encouraging social justice groups. There are a couple of ways to judge your community's success. Qualitatively, the best community happens when every single person can be their authentic and true self. My dream community is diverse in terms of ethnicity, age, religion, and everything else. Even a technology group should have different experience levels, ages, backgrounds, and programming languages.

   Quantitatively, we look at repeat RSVPs. It's a simple metric, but if there are ten thousand people in a group and a different fifty attend each time, it's not an interesting community. If there are eighteen people in a book club, and thirteen show up every time and two or three new people attend each time, that is a huge success. That means these people are showing up time after time, they're building deep relationships, and those relationships are translating into their wanting to come back. Ideally, there's new blood coming in, too, because community is always strengthened by new people joining.

6. *Look at new customers and revenue sources.* Make sure you're out looking at new customers and revenue sources as part of your pivot. For us, we have a business called Meetup Pro, where companies such as Amazon, Google, and Microsoft each have hundreds of different Meetup groups. Many founders also create a Meetup group to build community around their product.

   We leaned even more aggressively into B2B as part of our pivot. We also endeavored to identify different groups around topics of interest, then engage those groups and drive access to anyone in that community as an additional growth source.

Challenge 41: How to evaluate if a pivot is successful

While the pivot to online events proved valuable to me as a leader, did it prove valuable to Meetup?

How do you know whether you made the right decision?

Decision 41: Sometimes it's easy. You have no other choice but to pivot. If you don't pivot, you die.

Sometimes evaluating a major decision can take a decade and at other times you get clear signs that you were right very quickly. In our pivot, we knew immediately we made the right call.

In the twelve months after the start of the pandemic, Meetup had more than 15 million attendees to 2.5 million online Meetup events—from zero online events in our first eighteen years. Our members were craving community even more than before the pandemic. Loneliness was at an all-time high, and Meetup could be an all-time solution for the world's social isolation. After losing nearly $50 million in the previous four years, Meetup has been profitable every month since the sale of the company.

Meetup also began to take the lead in meeting again in person, once we understood how to do so safely. We started with New Zealand, Australia, Hong Kong, South Korea, and Singapore—the countries that had beaten back COVID—and we saw Meetup events and attendees quickly start to meet and then exceed their pre-coronavirus levels. We moved to *Europe and then to the United States.* Our marketing team monitored the rising and falling of COVID cases across every major city and country in the world. As cases increased, we would pull back marketing spend. As cases started to decrease again, we would increase spend. We created incredibly complex financial and marketing models that analyzed which topics were most interesting in which season and in which location, and how each country was being impacted by COVID, to determine where to market and to always encourage safe behaviors by our millions of members. Some topics grew enormously—spirituality, wellness, cycling, tennis, and the outdoors. Others were decimated such as any contact sports (like basketball or rugby) and large conference-like indoor tech events.

Our online meetings, nonetheless, continue to remain steady and, despite the vaccine, will grow. The greatest fear by our organizers is that we will eliminate online events once the pandemic has abated. I have told our organizers that we will always have online events for a number of reasons:

1. *Global brand building:* If, for example, a book author wanted to use Meetup to create a community around their brand, then in the past they would have had to create two thousand different communities in two thousand different cities. They can now create one online group and have members and a following anywhere in the world.
2. *Access to millions of Meetup events:* If someone lives in a rural village and wants to learn a new language or technical process, that person would have had access to those Meetup groups only

in their town—and some small towns had very few Meetup groups. Every person in the world now has access to the same learning opportunities as individuals in the largest cities. Online events can break down the barriers to equitable learning opportunities.

3. *A community of niche interests:* If someone is interested in collectible 1980s *Star Wars* action figures or, God forbid, has a rare disease and is looking for a support group, that person now has a global and therefore far larger group of people with whom to build an online community than just the people in their vicinity.

For each of these reasons and others, online events will forever continue. The backbone, however, of Meetup must return to in-person events. There is something special about getting together in person. Post-pandemic, online events and online connecting and dating are going to continue. Companies able to capitalize on people's behaviors and comfort level with videoconferencing are going to continue as well.

If not for the pandemic, we would never have offered amazing experiences for millions of people. The pandemic has created the opportunity to accelerate something that, frankly, we should have done much earlier, but there was too strong of a cultural taboo for us to have addressed it in the past.

Such taboos are not inherent in an organization. They only seem to be. They are de facto, not de jure; that is, they accrete over time like mold, they aren't designed. You can get past them so long as you trust in your mission, the actual designs of your business. It is your job as a leader to constantly question those cultural taboos and ask others if they still serve their intended purpose or if there even was an intended purpose to begin with.

This enabled us overcome our final challenges.

Challenge 42: Planning for the future

As a CEO, I spent an enormous amount of time trying to keep WeWork or other potential owners from destroying the soul and future of Meetup. With that constraint removed and with an owner who really supported what I wanted Meetup to do, I was faced with asking myself, almost for the first time, "What did I want Meetup to become?"

That was a lot harder to decide than what I knew I didn't want Meetup to be.

Decision 42: Keep working on your purpose.

When George Floyd was brutally murdered, we cried together as a Meetup community. We supported one another and we also began to realize that this tragedy, too, could be a galvanizing force for our company. As a leaner, independent company, we could act quickly. We developed a six-step action plan to use Meetup's power to drive racial equality. At the same time we used this as an opportunity to dig deeply into what Meetup stood for and to utilize the good that Meetup could provide in Black Lives Matter as an accelerator for the greater good we could provide to future movements.

The six steps:

1. *Donation:* Work with our Meetup in Color ERG (employee resource group) to identify the most critical organizations for Meetup donations. Our new chairman, Kevin Ryan, then offered to match dollar-for-dollar all donations we made for this cause.
2. *Employee support:* Build a resource hub, learning materials, and speakers related to diversity and inclusion.

3. *Drive voting:* Take charge of our country's direction, in partnership with the nonprofit When We All Vote, as part of the upcoming November 2020 election.
4. *Member education:* Bring BLM dialogue to millions of our members and organizers and create an ongoing monthly Meetup Live series: Dismantling Social Injustice.
5. *Community building:* Offer Meetup Pro, our highest-end product, for free to any groups who want to leverage it to build racial equality.
6. *Black Lives Matter awareness:* Drive millions of visitors toward groups and events that are driving change.

As I thought about what we want Meetup to be after the sale, the dual global events around the coronavirus and Black Lives Matter crystallized our focus. We needed to double down on the soul of our company. Our mission of "empowering personal growth through real human connections" is what needed to be our priority. If we use our soul as our guide, we will both unlock our company's potential and enable every employee to reap the financial benefits that will come only from prioritizing our soul.

It was now December 2020. I had to create a strategic plan for our upcoming year. I created the 2019 strategic plan (my first) on an abridged time frame because our employees demanded a quick direction from their new CEO. I created the 2020 strategic plan in the middle of a sales process to placate our WeWork overlords and potential buyers, and it was quickly thrown out the window with the pandemic. I needed to create a plan that wasn't about impressing anyone but was about providing a true direction for Meetup. Interestingly, that is a lot harder to do.

Challenge 43: Creating a strategic plan

How do you create a plan that is inspiring but achievable, focused but flexible, and realistic but aspirational?

Decision 43: Look to the past.

Let history guide you, because as the saying goes, "History never repeats itself, but it does often rhyme."

I shared with employees that Meetup has an opportunity to drive growth based on lessons we could take from the dual tragedies in the late 1910s: the Spanish flu and World War I. After a stress-filled, physically and emotionally challenging period that saw millions of Americans and tens of millions of individuals across the globe suffer immeasurably, the United States and world entered a new decade that represented the greatest growth period in our history: the Roaring Twenties.

In the late 1910s, people couldn't leave their homes for fear of disease, they were bombarded with political schisms the world had never seen, anxiety and stress were higher than in a century—sound familiar?—and then the war ended and herd immunity finally defeated the Spanish flu. The deep desire of people to get out of their homes, go to parties (the '20s were roaring for a reason!), attend conferences and events—do the exact opposite of what they weren't allowed to do in the years past—was palpable.

Enter 2021.

Almost exactly a century later, we suffer similar societal ills. And in the years ahead, we will rejoice in the same societal ways. Community and in-person interactions will be more important than ever. While there's a lot of talk about everything changing, the human need for connection is deep-rooted and fundamental. Individuals will be seeking new experiences, the pursuit of passions, and more connections than ever before. And Meetup has the opportunity to be at the center of it all.

I explained that Meetup has the potential to be the single largest beneficiary of the tragedy of COVID-19 since there will be a renewed vigor and desire for people to get off their butts and back out into the world. It is dangerous to think of any silver linings out of the global pandemic, and we need to be careful here, but at Meetup we can and will support the return back to community. The company's founding was due to perhaps the other greatest tragedy of our lifetimes, 9/11. Perhaps it shouldn't be that tragedy strengthens us, but the universe works in mysterious ways, and I tend to be a strong believer in what doesn't destroy us makes us stronger.

I shared how excited I was about the eventuality of history repeating itself and that we'll be back to the roaring '20s again (with hopefully a better ending this time around). It may take another six months, nine months, or maybe even a year, but we know it will roar. And the work that Meetup is doing now, in fixing our platform and making incremental user improvements, will accelerate Meetup's growth when the roaring starts and will enable Meetup to roar along with it.

Fixing our platform and removing tech debt would ensure we are using modern technology to move faster and deliver customer improvements. It would free us from the shackles of a legacy system written at a time before we could rely on third-party tools to handle core functionality. It opens up the opportunity to experiment with new ways of creating events. And it allows for an industry-standard approach to engaging with users via email, push notifications, and in-app messaging. Each of these is reason alone that fixing our platform will unlock Meetup growth, but compounded, the results will be exceptional.

I explained that I also believe that the pandemic has fundamentally— and forever—changed how people will work with each other. Long gone are the majority of employees working in an office from "9 to

5" (as if the "9" and "5" weren't already gone with the last generation anyway). In the new era of work, we'll be "work floaters," especially among the tech community, which Meetup most serves. People may "float" into the office for a few hours a day or a few hours a week, or not at all. Employees of companies (and most acutely Gen Zers and millennials) will, sadly, no longer enjoy the social fabric and rich community they had through work in the past. They won't be interacting dozens of times together in person, heading to coffees, lunches, and the pub after work in the same ways as before COVID-19. Their most meaningful community—the one with their trusted colleagues, who have now become more like friends—will be torn asunder.

Enter Meetup.

People's thirst for community will not abate, but their greatest enabler of community, especially for people early in their careers, will have been diminished. Meetup can help fill that void. Meetup will be more important in a world where community is no longer at work as it once was. We have seen similar transformations happen over the last century. Community transitioned from church and other places of worship to other societal groups. Another community transition then happened from PTAs and block parties to office outings and work parties. The transition will now be from work communities to identity and interest communities. It is in our hands to directly impact what future communities will be. Sorry, Facebook, online isn't enough. And the platform that is the best at facilitating those in-person communities, where people *show up*, is Meetup.

These dual macro trends, of an outpouring of desire for in-person connectedness and the schism of work leading to the growth of identity and interest communities, is why I am so excited about Meetup's future. We couldn't control the short-term devastation that COVID has had on Meetup's ecosystem, but we can take advantage of these macro trends to realize serious growth and success in late 2021 and beyond.

I told the team that we now have a deep understanding of our ecosystem and the value of each action within it. After careful analysis and in the spirit of our value #TrustInTransparency, we focused our 2021 efforts as a company on three activities: RSVPers to events (growing demand), new events created (growing event supply), and new organizers (even more event supply). While each of these is critical, the primary focus of our organization in 2021 was on driving new users to our platform to attend more events, and within that, our primary growth was accelerating our three hundred thousand–plus monthly registrations to their first RSVP. When we focus on our members, everyone wins.

I explained that Meetup will no doubt succeed because it is inherently a growth flywheel that doesn't depend on outside sources of growth but can "feed itself" to grow on a consistent basis as it always had in the past. The company doesn't need WeWork. We don't need our board. Hell, we don't even need the CEO. Some companies are transcendent and infinite, and that would be the case with Meetup.

I then ended my speech by explaining that Meetup would succeed because each of our employees can feel how much the world needs Meetup and knows how each will contribute to driving growth and company success for years to come.

Our employees felt inspired and further renewed both because we shut the company down for the last ten days of the year (sometimes you need to force people to take time off to avoid burnout!) and because the vaccine seemed to be the savior that would bring in-person connecting to heights it had never achieved before. And so far, we have been right.

In sum, in the final chapter of your leadership journey, you almost always will need to pivot your company. Lethargy as a leader is too dangerous. Here's how you do it:

- Follow my six principles of a successful pivot: (1) remain grounded in your mission; (2) support your pivot with best practices to help users transition; (3) understand how the pivot affects your ecosystem so you can react accordingly; (4) focus on future opportunities, not just present challenges; (5) leverage your data to understand your community; and (6) look to add new customers and revenue sources.
- Evaluate the success of your pivot. You might get clear signs quite quickly.
- Plan for your future after the pivot. This is where you double down on your mission.
- Create a new strategy. Let your gut and history guide you.

EPILOGUE

MEETING THE CHALLENGE EVERY DAY

It has now been more than a year since we were acquired. The pandemic is responsible for the death of millions of lives and has destroyed the emotional health of hundreds of millions more. While the year was a difficult one for both Meetup and my family, I consider myself to be fortunate to have had my entire family get COVID, survive with no lingering effects, and be vaccinated. We've worked from home and struggled with loneliness but have been there for our children and friends, each of whom have struggled, but also grown, during this difficult year. We've grown as a family by playing more nightly board games than I ever could have imagined. I've deepened my relationships with neighbors who, like me, hang out outside and take frequent walks. I've taken hundreds of walks with friends and family this year and appreciated the value of community more than ever.

When I had COVID and was forced to quarantine for nearly two weeks, I struggled. I'm not someone who is able to be locked up and still be in a happy place. It was the bitter wintertime in New York, I was sick and unable to leave my home, and when the quarantine finally ended, I needed to make a change. I was flooded with antibodies and decided to book a flight to Miami. I needed to imbue some spontaneity and happiness into my life, so I knocked off a personal bucket-list item and bleached my hair and went bright purple. No wash off. Permanent. Walking around Miami with my purple hair was exactly what I needed to heal after COVID. I had dozens of strangers strike up conversations. I hadn't met a new person in nearly a year and I was able to enjoy that special spark that happens when meeting someone whom you may think you could have little in common with but discover you have many of the same challenges and dreams. My newly colored hair shocked friends and our board in Zoom meetings. Many thought I was officially in midlife-crisis mode but understood the need to just do something silly and different in a time when we have all been surrounded by much pain and sameness.

Challenge 44: Leading your personal life

How do you take what you've learned from your career and apply it to your personal life?

Decision 44: Just relax and be yourself.

Being a leader involves tons of growth. You'll learn a lot. You'll meet interesting people. You'll achieve unbelievable success and suffer devastating failure. So when you have time off, you need a break. Just relax. Be yourself. You've already learned the lessons you need to. Be you, and you'll do well.

Three stories stand out most about my two-month (until I finally got a haircut) purple hair experience:

I was in Miami, running along the boardwalk, and arrived at South Pointe Park. There I saw a few hundred millennials singing and dancing in the waves in a silent disco. I gingerly walked over and saw a woman close to my age watching. I could tell that she wanted in but was uncomfortable participating by herself. The Meetup mantra is to welcome everyone immediately to an event, so with my newfound purple-hair confidence, I told her that we both needed to join the silent disco. We danced and sang our hearts out as the waves crashed against us. It was spiritual, uplifting, and cathartic. It further drove home the power of in-person events over online experiences. Afterward, I spent an hour hearing the life stories of others who attended the silent disco. That never could have happened online.

As an Orthodox Jew, I often wear a yarmulke. There aren't many purple-haired guys with a yarmulke, but there are many people in Miami who have either colored hair or wear a yarmulke. Being perceived as a religious traditionalist on the one hand and rugged individualist on the other presented a juicy dichotomy to those whom I passed on the streets. Many religious Jews' mouths were agape upon seeing me, and I could dispel others' preconceptions of the more traditional nature of Orthodox Jews. I had so many people stop me and comment on my hair and start up a conversation. Often, it broke down preconceived notions about religious people, and that dialogue was an opportunity to educate and eliminate certain stereotypes.

Upon coming home, I learned a lot about different people's reactions to my hair. I had a few guys tell their wives that they were worried about me. One wife actually called my wife and expressed sincere concern for me. I also had other friends and neighbors who just stopped me in the street or gave me high fives out of nowhere. It was such a source of joy and happiness. I learned a lot about people's reactions to people who may look different than them. Some reactions were great while others were troubling. I can only imagine how others feel who look, act, or dream in ways counter to the majority and who may or may not be able to express those dreams.

I've learned a lot about myself and leadership generally during the pandemic and can reflect on those lessons in the context of the key principles in this book:

- **Be kind:** Loneliness is an epidemic that had a compounding effect on those suffering during the pandemic. My heart deeply goes out to all those who live alone and were alone and isolated during this time. My two-week quarantine was torture; I can't comprehend how painful isolation was for tens of millions.

- **Be confident:** As the leader of a company that was dependent on meeting up but couldn't, it would have been easy for me to get pessimistic about Meetup's future. As I received reports every day for four hundred consecutive days showing declines relative to pre-pandemic levels, I could have been embittered and despondent. One of our executives in fact became just that, and we agreed that he needed to leave. I didn't let that happen to me, however. I knew that the magnifying glass is always on the CEO, and if I didn't maintain that same energy and confidence in our future, despite wave after wave of the pandemic, all would lose confidence as well.

- **Be bold:** I've always believed that the greatest risk is taking no risks. Friends of mine who chose to further isolate themselves and eliminate any risk of getting COVID have suffered deeply emotionally, physically, and psychologically. We need to be careful, but we need to be emboldened to live life despite the real risks.

- **Expand your options:** I have never run so much in my life. Although gyms were shut down, I have never swum or exercised as much as I did during the pandemic. My mental health and sanity were dependent on exercise and despite, or actually, because of the pandemic, I am in better shape than I have been in years.

- **Be long-term focused:** As I mentioned earlier, the pandemic gave Meetup and many other companies an opportunity to step back and focus less on short-term growth or WeWork-driven Hail Mary projects and more on removing tech debt and culture debt. The time spent on building a robust and data-driven planning process and enabling Meetup to iterate quickly will pay massive dividends in the years ahead. I genuinely believe that Meetup will succeed because of the pandemic, not despite it.

• **Be honest:** I live a life of extreme privilege, and while I recognized and appreciated it in the past, it is no more evident than during this last year. While many people of color have had a profoundly challenging year and others in the service sector lost their jobs and are struggling to put food on the table, my greatest misery was boredom. I've learned to be more honest with myself and others about how unfair life is for many and the criticality of those in privilege to do all we can for those who are not. The pandemic greatly magnified the inequalities that were already an enormous chasm.

• **Be speedy:** As a college professor who had planned an in-person student gathering, I was eligible to get the COVID vaccine in January 2021. Optionality! I decided to wait a few weeks to be sure not to take the spot of an elderly or infirmed individual but was able to be one of the earlier individuals vaccinated. By being speedy, I was able to hug my mom, spend more time helping friends, and live life fuller and quicker than many of my colleagues. There was no reason to wait, and when there is no reason to wait, just do it.

• **Be pragmatic:** Our executives and managers who were able to prioritize taking care of their own emotional health and physical needs during the pandemic thrived and served as a source of inspiration for their teams. Other leaders were less pragmatic and didn't appreciate the criticality of taking care of themselves so they could be an overflowing cup for others. As their stress, pessimism, and fear of the virus continued, they were unable to lead effectively and ultimately left the company.

- **Do what's right for the business:** Through the entire year, not once did we say, "What does the board want?" In fact, our employees frequently asked me that question and my answer was always the same: "Our board wants us to figure out what we want to do and prioritize that." There were no politics, no need to rationalize specific actions; we had the trust of our investors, and our leadership trusted our managers. We followed the principle of the "upside-down organizational chart." The individual on the bottom of the chart, me, is responsible for supporting those above, and that scaled up to the rest of the organization. And that is how we ensured we were doing what was right for the business and not what was right for employee happiness or board priorities.

- **Work for your employees:** Communication is hard enough when a team is all in one location, but it is far harder when all employees are remote. With savings we gained from having no rent, we decided to prioritize overcommunication and investing in employee wellness. I had weekly meetings with all managers and monthly all-hands with employees. We ended every executive team meeting with this agenda item: "What do we need to share with our employees based on what we discussed today?" We made every Wednesday Wellness Wednesday and hired yoga instructors and meditation leaders and other advisors to help our stressed employees find the best ways to take care of themselves and others. We worked for our employees, and in turn, they worked incredibly hard for Meetup.

- **Be surprised only about being surprised:** Meetup's acquirer, Kevin Ryan, has been the greatest partner I could have hoped for after a year of working together. Kevin and the rest of the board have been supportive of investing in Meetup's long-term health while being appropriately demanding that we be financially responsible and ambitious in our post-pandemic goals. I have not had a single surprise from our board in the year that we have partnered together.

A friend of mine suffered psychologically and emotionally during COVID and had to be taken to a hospital. Upon meeting the chaplain, she said to him, "When you're in a sailboat in the middle of a storm, what should you do?" The answer: "Don't freeze. You have a higher likelihood of tipping over and drowning. You need to bob and weave through the chaos of the waves as your best chance of staying afloat." For much of Meetup's time at WeWork and then during the pandemic, we were unable to freeze. We needed to keep responding to the situation, bobbing, weaving, and dancing to stay afloat. And we did.

In the year since the sale, Meetup has been cash flow positive every month after having never been cash-flow positive in any month in the three years prior. We decided to double down during the pandemic in emphasizing the importance of community and giving our organizers and members the tools to be more effective community leaders. Our blog, *Community Matters*, now has more than two million subscribers. We started producing a twice-a-week event called Meetup Live that is now Meetup's largest group with more than two hundred thousand event attendees and one hundred thousand members. We started a podcast called *Keep Connected* to hear the inspirational stories of how anyone can start a community and change the lives of others.

And now we are seeing the growth. Although every key company metric had precipitously declined a year ago, we are now seeing the number of new subscribers, events created, and RSVPs to those events increasing 40, 50, 60, 70 percent from our low point. The world is getting slowly vaccinated, and with each injection of hope that the vaccine instills, it is another person who can safely get back to hugging their loved ones and enjoying time, in person again, with friends.

When I was younger, I remember hearing a rabbi tell a friend that they hoped the next time they spoke, they would hear that they had a "boring life." I was incensed. What kind of a blessing is it to tell someone that you hoped that their life was boring! I wanted a life of adventure and excitement that changed every day. Now I don't. The year after Meetup's sale has been boring. And thank God for that. Some days I even will take a short afternoon nap. Boring is good. Boring means that I don't need to wake up in a cold sweat each day wondering what crazy idea WeWork may have in running our business or selling us. Boring means that we can focus on what is holding us back and not chase growth for growth's sake, but use the year to fix our tech infrastructure, rebuild our culture, and prepare for the growth we are now experiencing one year after the sale. I would give a blessing that every CEO have a boring time, or at least a period of time that is boring in order to focus on longer-term priorities.

The power of in-person connecting was further cemented when I taught my entrepreneurship class at Columbia during the pandemic. Teaching a course once a year has been a passion and highlight of my life for the last six years. Six years ago, my wife asked me what I wanted to do after I retire, and I told her I wanted to teach at a university. Her follow-up question was, "So why aren't you doing that now?" Probably my greatest joy outside of family has been the classes I first taught at Pace University and now teach at Columbia. My students' energy and enthusiasm for learning about business, strategy, and startups makes me a better person and leader. But this semester was different. I didn't enjoy it. Teaching through Zoom felt more like a perfunctory task than building a real connection with students.

I felt as if I were going through the motions, trying to engage the students with polls, break-out rooms, and my typical odd antics, but it wasn't the same as in-person teaching. After being fully vaccinated, I told the students that we should meet in Manhattan's Central Park where we could see each other in person and connect. And since that one meeting with about twenty students, teaching on Zoom has been transformed. It has been interesting to note that working through Zoom was not difficult for me since I had already established in-person relationships with many Meetuppers, and it was only after I had an in-person connection with my students that I was able to enjoy our classes later over Zoom. This again brought home for me the power and criticality of in-person connecting and what Meetup does for millions of people around the world. If I only partially appreciated the importance of IRL ("in real life") before COVID, I am a deep devotee of it today.

In this book, I wrote about the importance of being bold, taking action, and putting oneself in a position to "get lucky." And this has been exactly what has happened in the year since Meetup's sale. At one point in time, I was certain WeWork's eventual buyer would fire me. I had carelessly made clear on LinkedIn that I was open to learning about new opportunities. In the few days that this notification was live, I was approached by Riverside, a major private equity firm, to be an operating partner. We built a relationship during the ensuing discussions, I informed them that I would be staying on at Meetup, but they asked me to join the board of Soothe, the largest wellness platform for in-person massage therapists. It was my first board position and a result of the Meetup sale.

Another private equity firm who was strongly considering buying Meetup and with whom we engaged in numerous conversations acquired a major e-commerce floral business. After learning about my experience as a former executive at 1-800-Flowers.com and getting to know me during the Meetup sale process, they asked me to join FTD's board of directors as well. Another relationship from the Meetup sale process introduced me to a nonprofit organization with which I am now deeply involved. Meeting the hundreds of venture capital and private equity leaders during Meetup's sale has engendered relationships and conversations that I am now also bringing back to Meetup as meaningful business development opportunities. We're talking with dozens of other large organizations about ways in which Meetup can help their organizations and vice versa, and most of those relationships are a result of executives and leaders whom I met during the sale process. Relationships matter, and it's important to continue to cultivate them, not just when you need them.

One of my least favorite interview questions was always, "Where do you see yourself in five to ten years?" My take: Anyone who knows where they see themselves isn't someone I'd like to hire. Our careers bob, weave, and pivot through the storm of life and no one knows their futures. We plan and God laughs, and we can be only more sure of this today, after the pandemic. As for my own future, I intend to stay at Meetup for as long as I feel I am an asset to the company. I don't believe I will take on another corporate role after my time at Meetup is done. After this experience, I feel ready to move onto the next chapter of my life, whatever that may be, and I am thoroughly excited about it since I have no idea what it will bring. I'll likely use my experience to advise other leaders through teaching, mentoring, and serving on boards. I won't be another CEO.

As for Meetup, our future for the next many years is incredibly exciting. We now have the luxury to focus not on our short-term survival, but on the next pivot that will unlock far greater impact for the company. We're exploring a tremendous number of growth ideas to answer some of the following questions:

- Meetup has driven tens of thousands of marriages. Are we a better dating solution than Tinder? Can Meetup Singles build deep connections?
- Should we return to the way we grew up nearly twenty years ago and seed tens of millions of Meetup-created topics in all

193 countries we serve to dramatically increase growth outside of the United States?

- We never could get a true read on enabling organizers to make organizing on Meetup a full-time profession. Can we test this and avoid the public relations disaster of the past?
- Is there a path to a freemium model where there is a lite version of organizing at no cost that would unlock millions of potential new organizers?
- What is the most important investment we can make in our community tools to ensure that our members can build meaningful relationships and real communities with each other in a world where community at work and home has been decimated?

The one thing we do know for certain is that we won't attempt to pursue all these ideas simultaneously but will select one and put everything behind that one. Focus wins. This book comes out during Meetup's twentieth anniversary, and the next twenty years should prove more exciting to the company's future than even our first.

What I've learned already, and what I hope you've learned from this book, I summarized during a speech at UC Berkeley's Haas School of Business while Meetup was being sold. I shared many of the stories in this book and at the end shared a few takeaways related to being an influencer. I implored each student to understand how influential they can be in their own lives—both personally and professionally. **Be bold. Be kind.** And never give up. I had learned these lessons early in my career and they were critical to our success at Meetup. Here were a few of the key messages I shared:

1. *Never underestimate your ability to have a massive influence on your future.* In many ways, this is the theme of this book. Too often individuals give up their agency and leave their future happiness

in the hands of others, whether from fear of failure (if this applies to you, then know you are in the company of thousands of leaders), general laziness, or distraction from the many other parts of our lives. But our personal happiness and careers are too important to leave in the hands of anyone but ourselves.

Never underestimate how influential you can be in making an important decision. At the same time, once that decision is made, be sure you also "disagree and commit." Organizations—this is also true for marriages—can't function effectively if there is resentment after a decision is made.

2. *Strong relationships can drive massive influence and less rational decisions.* When WeWork president Artie Minson first told me about the Meetup sale, he encouraged me to talk with anyone with whom I had a past relationship and attempt a management buyout. He was rooting for me because of the relationship we had forged in the prior year. Kevin Ryan made the unlikely decision to acquire Meetup despite having conducted less diligence on the company than more than fifty other suitors. Deep relationships will enable your influence to massively expand.

   The relationships that I developed later, during the sales process, have also had a profound impact on my career. I had met the founders of a private equity firm that acquired a major e-commerce business. We built a great relationship and they asked me to be on their board as well. I built relationships with more than one hundred venture capital and private equity firms through the sales process, and while leading Meetup is more than a full-time job, I am confident that these relationships will present additional surprise opportunities.

3. *Always "be in the game" so you can have an influence. Optionality is a primary goal in making your decisions.* I refused to surrender

my agency in driving Meetup's future. As long as I could have a seat at the table, I knew I'd be able to influence the final outcome. Optionality is one of the most powerful capabilities while also often the least prioritized. I always tell my students that when choosing a career, they should focus on the choice that will **expand their options** as much as possible for future decisions as their careers progress. Life is a series of decisions, and your ability to make decisions that expand rather than constrict your future options is often the path to greater happiness later in life.

4. *Never fear failing. Fear not trying.* Whether it was how I was parented—as much of life is—or due to a potentially malfunctioning amygdala (the fear region of one's brain), I find fear to be one of the greatest contributors to the lack of personal and career happiness. It is the greatest contributor to inertia. Failing presents the greatest gift. It shouldn't be feared, but embraced. Failing drives learning better than any other activity. I never understood why someone would fear what also represents the greatest opportunity for learning and growth. I have failed many times in the past and will inevitably fail many more in the future. Embrace it.

5. *Indirect influence can be more powerful than direct influence. Work through others to maximize impact.* During Meetup's sale process, I frequently had either Chad, Kevin, or others communicate directly with WeWork's team instead of myself. At the same time, WeWork often asked me to follow up with a party with whom they were speaking to explain why we could or couldn't accommodate a specific due diligence request. Knowing that often it is more about who the messenger is and not what the message is, is critical to effective persuasion. As a parent of three teenagers, I'm keenly aware that the same message from one party (me) can be rebuked but embraced if it comes from another (friend, sibling,

or grandparent). Understanding how to indirectly influence the outcome is a theme at the core of getting what you most desire. And getting what you most desire is the result of making smart decisions.

While buying this book was hopefully a smart decision, it is leveraging the lessons in your life and career that is the smartest decision. A startup CEO whom I have been mentoring was dealing with an incredibly complex situation with her board. She read an advance copy of the book and informed me that it served as a guide for her strategy with her board. To me, that is the ultimate reward and the reason for my writing this book.

Having read hundreds of business books and been personally influenced by only a handful of them, I ask that, before you close this book for good, write down the three takeaways that may be most helpful to you. Good luck, and I hope that your life's decisions will always be a source of excitement for what is ahead in your own personal journey.

GRATITUDE

The acknowledgments section at the start or end of a book never quite resonated with me. Acknowledging is transactional, sterile, and feels detached from the person doing the acknowledging. One of the most important words in the English language is *gratitude*. Gratitude is not transactional. It is transformative. Gratitude builds a deepened relationship between the giver and receiver. When you have gratitude, you build a muscle that influences your perspective on every life event. Most experiences are neither black nor white; the same experience can be seen as positive or negative, depending on the viewer. It is through the gratitude muscle that we develop a positive life lens.

When I was in college, I recall declaring to friends that I had decided that the meaning of life is to "find joy in day-to-day actions that drive long-term happiness." The goal is to set oneself up for future happiness and to enjoy the process of doing so. It wasn't to just have fun that served no future purpose and it certainly wasn't to experience short-term pain for a happiness payoff later.

Twenty-five years later, I still have the same goal. And for me, the path toward short-term joy and longer-term happiness is gratitude. Gratitude drives appreciation for each of the moments in life and helps ensure that we do not take them for granted. Pursuing happiness without gratitude is impossible. Gratitude is the framework that drives a broad perspective, humility, and relationships. If you lack gratitude, you will be in a never-ending cycle of searching for more rather than understanding the good you already have.

Every morning when I wake up and every evening before I go to sleep, I say a short gratitude prayer that has been said for millennia before me. It anchors me in how I start my day and precedes my dreams of the night.

I have so much gratitude to so many people both in my life and related to this book.

I have gratitude to my parents, Ellie and Kenneth (Z"L) Siegel, for striking the complicated balance between giving me space to fail and unconditional support when I did.

I have gratitude for two incredible in-laws, Carol and David Kaplan, who not only produced the greatest daughter ever (my wife) but are incredibly nonjudgmental of my shenanigans.

I have gratitude for my siblings, Laurie and Nathan Siegel; although we differ in many ways, we are forever joined in supporting one another.

I have gratitude for the many individuals who helped edit this book:

- Tim Burgard, Jeff Farr, Sicily Axton, Mike Bzozowski, and the HarperCollins team for their incredible direction, support, and belief in someone who has never written a text longer than his high school history paper.
- Stephen S. Power, an executive editor at Kevin Anderson & Associates, who took a draft as rough as five-day stubble and helped me organize it into forty-four decisions.
- Elliot Herzig, who sent me a cold email and subsequently spent dozens of hours reading, rereading, and making editorial suggestions.
- Michael Kellman, a close friend, who encouraged me to write a detailed manuscript after our many long walks discussing the WeWork sale.

- Kevin Ryan, for his hiring me more than twenty years ago and his ongoing mentorship and support in both life and this book. And oh, for also being the lead investor in the Meetup sale.
- The many Meetuppers who provided feedback to ensure the book's accuracy: Giff Constable, David Diesenhouse, Mary Garcia, Eileen Gilbertson, Greg Giusti, Gwynn Krueger, Jeanine Mioton, Daniel Pardes, Prerna Singh, Sach Sokol, and Ronlee Tehranian.
- The many friends, students, and former colleagues who encouraged, reviewed, and maintained my sanity in writing the book: Radha Agrawal, Tiffany Daenecke, Daniel Ben David, Tal Ben-Shahar, Johnny Boufarhat, Jon Brodsky, Guy Cohen, Adam Enbar, Sarah Friar, Evi Heilbrunn, Yuejia Jiang, Erica Keswin, Binna Kim, Donald Krueger, Daniel LaGrua, J.J. Lando, Jon Levy, Leigh Nusbaum, Jennifer Perciballi, Vibhav Prasad, Shlomo Ressler, Michael Schein, Caleb Silver, Dan Simon, Wendy Tsu, and Noam Wasserman.
- The managers and mentors I have had in my career have shaped my life and professional goals in ways that I can never repay, but for which I have eternal gratitude. From my first managers and mentors when fresh out of college, Edward Goldstein, Sam Marcus, and Karen Dowd, to the mentors through the rest of my career: David Rosenblatt, Kevin Ryan, Brian (Skip) Schipper, Melanie Hughes, Jim Rizzo, Jim McCann, Chris McCann, Charlie Fraas, Ben Wolin, Paul Slavin, Avrom Gilbert, David Jackson, Sarah Holloway, Eli Hoffman, Doug Leeds, Adam Roston, and Joey Levin, thank you for all you have taught me about being both a good person and strong leader and how each reinforces the other.

Last but not least, I have gratitude for my wonderful family. To my three children, Yair, Nadiv, and Marni, you are our life and we hope you continue to grow into the people you want to be. To Lara, you are my life's best decision.

APPENDIX 1:
TURNAROUND LESSONS FOR
LEADERS

While I still don't believe the change management needs for Meetup are complete, we are in a vastly better place than during our dark WeWork days. Here are some lessons on how to drive organizational success during the challenging times that you may face as a leader:

1. *Flat organizational structure:* As a leader, it's important to be extremely hands-on. There is no delegating during a challenge. If you have too many layers, cut them out. You need to be talking directly with each functional head and not relying on others to transmit information down. At one point, I had an impossible-to-manage twelve direct reports. But it worked and alignment was built faster.

2. *Drive, don't empower:* There is a time for leadership empowerment of teams (and that should almost always be the management style in a steady-state organization), but during challenges you need to listen and then tell. You cannot have teams self-manage their way out of it; there will be misalignment and poor prioritization.

3. *Overcommunicate:* For many months, I had a weekly all-hands meeting with all employees and another weekly all-hands with every manager. They were predominantly Q&A, and it was important to explain the context and reasons behind decisions I was making, since many more decisions were being directed than empowered.

4. *Employee exits are healthy:* Don't take it as a personal failure when a long-tenured employee exits. There are more positives than losses in clearing out any historic naysayers and bringing in solution-oriented new hires.

5. *Replace the exec team:* I know this is harsh, but challenging times often require a nearly complete leadership change. The sooner a CEO realizes the impossibility of turning a company around with the current executive team, the faster changes can begin to have an impact. Through best intentions, many new CEOs give their new management teams the benefit of the doubt. After a few months they realize that being "nice" resulted only in their personal ineffectiveness in changing a company's culture and management practices.

6. *A rallying cry can be very effective:* Find a message that resonates with your employees and speaks to their noble cause and drive it home over and over again. We wrote a new company mission: "to empower personal growth through real human connections." I must have said it hundreds of times and I tried to connect every action back to our mission.

7. *Small wins:* They create momentum and optimism that motivate an individual toward that next—and next—small win. Each win—2 percent here, 1.5 percent there—compounds, and many of these wins add up to meaningful progress. Prior to Meetup's sale out of WeWork, small wins were perceived by WeWork leadership (Adam Neumann) as "the domain of the weak." Ambitious individuals looked for the home run. Meetup was highly discouraged from focusing on small wins that had a high likelihood of success that could compound into meaningful progress. No more. As Confucius said, "The person who moves a mountain begins by carrying away small stones."

8. *Milestones:* Set and communicate realistic milestones about how long it will likely take until employees are "feeling the momentum."

In a particularly challenging situation, it will never take less than nine to twelve months, and more often will take multiple years. Be sure the team is geared up for it and that realistic expectations are set. Due to my overconfidence and "need to please," I did a terrible job in understanding and effectively communicating this principle.

9. *Culture debt:* Most importantly, many companies believe that one of the greatest challenges in a tech-driven change is tech debt. Tech debt disenables the ability to fix serious user experience flaws. However, a far greater problem is culture debt. In a turn-around, there is significant culture debt. The company culture may be burnt out, apathetic, indifferent to business success, or all of these (as at Meetup). Acknowledge it and fix this fast, as you cannot turn a company around unless you have addressed its legacy culture debt as the primary cause of tech debt.

APPENDIX 2:
SAMPLE LAYOFF SPEECH

Whatever you do, don't use this speech.

If there could be anything worse than a boss who spends years praising you, then lays you off one morning by reading legally approved language off a card provided by HR (and reading it to you over the phone, no less), it's probably finding out you're being laid off with someone else's layoff speech.

So make the speech your own. Put things in your own words. That's what matters. This is just the order and tone of things from the speech I had given.

Everyone—

- OK, I'm sharing something today that is very difficult.
- There is no easy way to say this, so I am going to come right out with it—
- Today we are going to say goodbye to about 10 percent of our team.

(pause to let that sink in)

- I was originally planning on sending an email, but I decided against it since that's not Meetup.

- We are an IRL company, and whether it is for good or for challenges like to today, we are going to face it in a direct, transparent way.
- So I need to read this because it is important that I get this message exactly right.
- Please excuse me for doing it this way . . .

I joined Meetup because of a passionate belief in our business, our community, and the huge impact Meetup has on people's lives. I'm pretty sure that's why we all joined Meetup.

A few weeks ago at our Org Structure All-Hands, I talked about the seven-step process to changing the company. Step one was the new structure, and step two was to identify the people to support that structure.

Through hundreds of hours of conversations with you, really examining the business, close consultation with the lead team, and bringing together nearly one hundred people for our strategy workstreams, this important, but difficult, decision was made. And it is a very important one and not taken lightly.

We are saying goodbye to fellow Meetuppers who have made a meaningful impact on our business.

For me, this is the first time in my entire career that I have had to oversee an action such as this, but unfortunately we felt we have no choice for the sake of Meetup's viability. Simply put, this was a last resort. These changes are being made to ensure we are more focused and the team we have in place is directly aligned with our company priorities—also known as The Big Three (revenue, customer experience, and new business model).

OK, so next steps:

1. People who are leaving us today will receive a calendar invite within the next five to ten minutes after this meeting, letting them know their next steps.

(Short pause)

2. People who are *not* impacted will get an email with an outline for the rest of the day.

(Short pause)

3. Today at 2 p.m. ET, we'll come back together for an all-hands where we will discuss the changes, and most importantly, give you an opportunity to ask questions.

(Short pause)

I know this is a lot to process. There's no ideal way to do this.

Two final thoughts: One, it's important to me that we don't shy away from your questions about it, and, two, that we treat those who are leaving today with integrity, thoughtfulness, and empathy.

(Pause)

Thanks for your time. I'm going to excuse you now.

(Stay onstage while everyone exits.)

APPENDIX 3:
SAMPLE SUCCESSION EMAIL

Whether you're fired or let go in some fashion (the most likely end of your tenure, it's sad to say) or you leave for a new job (good luck!), it's your final responsibility to your employees that you set their new boss up for success. There's no reason they should suffer. So here in full is the email that Scott sent to welcome me to Meetup. Scott's email and embrace of me to his team was truly phenomenal, and I include his email to give you a model for writing one yourself. Remember: Be enthusiastic. Be professional. And be confident that you'll be remembered well by being generous during what is surely a trying time for you.

To: [Staff]
From: Scott
Subject: Welcome David Siegel, Meetup's new CEO

Hi team,

Big news! We found someone really good—and you'll meet him at noon ET today.

I met dozens of candidates.

David went through 26 meetings over three months.

David had the most passion for our mission, the highest energy, and the right approach for what Meetup needs today.

We wanted him, and he starts today!

So what does Meetup need today? And why is David the right leader for Meetup today?

You'll hear more at noon ET, but here's my summary . . .

Meetup needs someone right now who combines:

- a very methodical approach to caring for and growing our customer and member base

- an obsession for the people side: setting up teams to work better together

- experience navigating big companies to make an independent subsidiary successful

That's David. I expected we'd hire someone from one of the giant internet borgs—and we met plenty of those people. David's background was different. He spent the past twenty years leading teams and companies, proving himself as a leader who earns people's trust—and drives success.

Most recently, he was CEO of an IAC company called Investopedia, where he tripled revenue in three years by growing a subscription model (like Meetup) with a rich user-generated ecosystem (like Meetup). His team loved him.

When you spend time with him, it's clear how he makes companies more successful. He knows what he's not—he's not a software engineer or UI designer. He's an organizational design/engineering whiz with a focus on methodically growing Meetup activity and revenue. I went on a Meetup Crawl with him, he felt Meetuppy all along, and you'll sense his integrity, his heart, and his smarts.

Meetup CEO is the best job in the world, IMO. You get to focus on a critical mission: Bring millions of people together IRL to create community and opportunity; and you get to lead the most talented and passionate crew ever assembled to bring that kind of mission to life. It's been the ride of my life for me to serve in the role for almost 17 years.

Meetup CEO is also a really hard job, so I ask that you welcome David, hold him to the high expectations our mission deserves, have patience with him as he learns, and respect what he's here to do: David is here to make Meetup much more successful. "Change the Company" is a long-standing core value of ours because that's the way for any organism or organization to thrive, so I ask for your openness. That's one favor I ask of you.

I'm now moving into the role of chairman and what I want most is for David to succeed as CEO. The best way for a former CEO to respect the new one is to not get in that person's way—and to not confuse the team about who's in charge. So I'll go on sabbatical for 90 days, meeting regularly with David to help him.

Join me in welcoming David—and thanking him for taking this giant leap!

—Heif
Co-founder & Chairman

ABOUT THE AUTHOR

David Siegel is the CEO of Meetup, the largest platform for finding and building local communities. He has more than twenty years of experience as a technology and digital media executive, leading organizations through innovative product development, rapid revenue growth, and digital traffic acceleration. Prior to joining Meetup, David was CEO of Investopedia and, before that, president of Seeking Alpha. David holds a BA in Philosophy, Politics & Economics and an MBA from the University of Pennsylvania. He is an adjunct professor at Columbia University, where he teaches strategic planning and entrepreneurship, and has been published most notably in *Harvard Business Review*, *Sloan Management Review*, *Business Insider*, and *Entrepreneur*. He hosts the podcast *Keep Connected*, a Top 25–ranked CEO podcast that is dedicated to the power of community. He lives in White Plains, New York, with his wife and three teenage children. In his spare time, he likes to pop in on Meetup events.